The Bowler's Guide

USBC
United States Bowling Congress

CONTENTS

1. **The Evolution**
of Bowling........................ **06**

Early Bowling History.............................06
History of Tenpin Bowling in the U.S........07
Membership and Rules-making
Organizations...08

2. **The Playing Field**............**10**

Bowling Centers.....................................10
The Lane...11
Lane Markings.......................................13
The Pins...14

3. **Personal**
Equipment........................ **15**

Bowling Balls...15
Bowling Shoes/Proper Clothing..............17

4. **Modern Rules**
Of Bowling....................... **18**

History and Formation
of Modern Rules....................................18
Modern Rules...19
Types of Bowling....................................21
Tournaments..23
Bowling Etiquette...................................25

5. **Preparing to Bowl**
and the Stance.............. **26**

Dynamic and Static
Stretching Exercises..............................26

Bowling Ball Safety................................27
Starting Position on the Approach............28

6. **The Basic Approach**....**30**

The Four-Step Approach.........................30
Follow Through.......................................31
Five-Step Approach................................31
Lane Targets..31

7. **The Release**...................... **32**

Wrist Positions.......................................32
Ball Rotation..32
Straight Ball...32
Basic Hook Release................................33
Basic Hook Release with
Finger and Wrist Rotation.......................33
Reverse Hook...33
The "No Thumb" Release.........................33
Loft..34
Common Release Problems.....................34

8. **Developing**
Consistency...................... **35**

Armswing...35
Shoulders/Torso.....................................35
Drifting..36
Types of Timing......................................37
Balance in the Finish Position.................37
Common Errors and Solutions................38

9. **Lane Conditions**............ **39**

Purposes of Lane Conditioners...............39
Lane Oil Patterns...................................40

10. Making Adjustments 42

The Starting Position 42
Adjustments with Feet 42
Altering the Release 43
Adjusting Speed 43
Altering the Ball Surface 44
Reasons to Make Adjustments 44

11. Spare Shooting 45

Step 1: Identify the Key Pin 45
Step 2: Aligning the Feet
on the Approach to a New
Starting Position 46
Step 3: Square the Body
to the Target on the Lane 46

12. The Mental Game 47

Staying Positive 47
Visualization and
Positive Mental Imagery 47
Focus on the Process,
Not Outcome 47
Controlling Emotions 48
Setting Goals 48

13. Adaptive Skills 49

Wheelchair Bowling 49
Visually-Impaired Bowlers 51
Other Adaptive Techniques
and Equipment 51

14. Youth and Seniors ... 52

Techniques for Young Bowlers 52
Two-handed Delivery 52
One-handed Delivery 54
Techniques for Senior Bowlers 55

15. National Organizations and Resources 57

International Bowling
Campus (IBC) 57
Other National Organizations 59

16. Career Opportunities in Bowling 60

Amateur Competition 60
Professional Competition 60
Industry Opportunities 61

17. Glossary of Bowling Terms 62

Book Design: Diana Bracken

Editor: Terry Bigham and Teresa Ross

Content: Nick Bohanan, David Garber, Bryan O'Keefe, Bob Learn Jr., Stephen Padilla and Teresa Ross

Photography: USBC Archives, Diana Bracken, and Ellman Photography

Special thanks to all of our models: Ben Brose, Brenda Edwards, Bailey Graham, Brooklyn Graham, Drew Johnson, Stephen Padilla, Kayla Shelley, Tyler Viator, Kayla Warren, Ryan Warren, Kristin Warzinski, Aubrey "Red" White, Betty White, Isaiah Willis

United States Bowling Congress

THE EVOLUTION OF BOWLING

Artist rendition of early Egyptian bowling.

Bowling has a long and rich history, and today it is one of the world's most popular sports. In the 1930s, British anthropologist Sir Flinders Petrie discovered a collection of objects in a child's grave from ancient Egypt that appeared to be an early form of bowling. The primitive objects included nine pieces of stone at which a stone "ball" was rolled, the ball having first to roll through an archway made of three pieces of marble.

If Sir Petrie was correct, then bowling's ancestry can be traced as far back as 5200 B.C. However, German historian William Pehle asserted that bowling began in his country about 300 A.D.

There also is substantial evidence that a form of bowling was fashionable in England in 1366, when King Edward III allegedly outlawed the game to keep his troops focused on archery practice. And it is almost certain that bowling was popular during the reign of Henry VIII.

Bowling at pins probably originated in ancient Germany, not as a sport but as a religious ceremony. Martin Luther is credited with settling on nine as the ideal number of pins.

By this time, there were many variations of "pin" games, and also of games in which a ball was thrown at objects other than pins.

One of the most eccentric games is still found in Scotland. The player swings a heavy ball with both hands between his legs and heaves it at the pins. In doing so, he "flops" onto the lane on his stomach. There were - and still are - many variations of bowling in Western Europe. Likely related are Italian bocce, French petanque and British lawn bowling.

indoor lanes were built throughout Manhattan and the Bronx and westward in Syracuse, Buffalo, Cincinnati, Chicago, Milwaukee and other cities with large German populations. Many were part of turnvereins – fraternal gymnastic societies – but they quickly spread to wide public usage.

Henry VIII and his courtiers at White Hall in 1530

History of tenpin bowling in the United States

After bowling moved throughout Europe and the Scandinavian countries, the game finally made it to the United States with English, Dutch and German settlers all having imported their own variations of the game.

The earliest known reference to bowling at pins in America was made by author Washington Irving in Rip Van Winkle (about 1818), in which he likens thunder to the sound of a ball rolling at pins.

By the mid-1830s, the game of ninepins was flourishing. It was then that the same scourge that struck lawn bowling in medieval England – gambling - became the evil of the American bowling scene. The situation became so critical in Connecticut that the state legislature passed an act in 1841 banning the game.

Myth has it that a quick-witted genius, to circumvent the prohibition which was supposed to refer only to the ninepin diamond formation, added the 10th pin and arranged them in the triangle used today.

Regardless of how tenpins came into being, the game became so popular by the mid-l9th century that

Top right photo: This is an unusual picture, for bowling in the 1860s was considered a disreputable sport and certainly not for the ladies. It had the same status as the pool room, a hangout for gamblers. This, then, must be a summer resort hotel or perhaps a privately-owned alley.

Photo below top right: Abraham Lincoln is believed to be the first American president who indulged in bowling. According to bowling historians, Lincoln enjoyed the good fellowship of the game. He relaxed his Civil War tensions with an occasional friendly game.

Beethoven Hall in New York City

Membership and rules-making organizations

American Bowling Congress

The American Bowling Congress was founded in 1895 with its roots traced to many people. One was Thomas Curtis, ABC's first president, who chaired several historic meetings which produced an organization which succeeded where others had failed.

The adoption of rules at the Sept. 9, 1895, meeting in New York City and, most important, the distribution by mail of nearly 1,000 copies to bowling groups in many parts of the United States, was the move which created interest and trust in the fledgling group. Within a few months, there were members in Buffalo (N.Y.), Cincinnati, Lowell (Mass.), Boston, Chicago, St. Louis, Wheeling (W.Va.), Kansas City and Quebec.

Many of today's rules and guidelines were established with the formation of the ABC.

Women's International Bowling Congress history

While women had been bowling in the latter half of the 19th century, the ABC was an organization for men. In 1916, women leaders from around the country formed what was to become the Women's International Bowling Congress.

There are many colorful stories about when women began bowling in the United States. At the turn of the century, women sneaked in with (or without) their husbands to try bowling. Often, they did so at the risk of their reputations.

Tales are told about women bowlers being screened from view behind partitions or drapes, or being allowed to bowl only when men were not using the alleys. Those were the days of high-button shoes, skirts to the ankles, cumbersome apparel and dingy parlors that were hardly appealing.

In 1915, avid bowler Ellen Kelly formed the St. Louis Women's Bowling Association. Buoyed by her success, she wrote to proprietors across the country asking for names of women who might be interested in a national organization of their own. She followed with letters to those women, urging the organization of local associations and offering advice on rules and establishing an organization.

Following the first women's national tournament in 1916, 40 women from 11 U.S. cities met at a bowling center in St. Louis and created the national organization that, after several name changes, became the Women's International Bowling Congress.

Young American Bowling Alliance history

Organized bowling for young people began in 1936 in Chicago when Milt Raymer, a high school teacher,

organized an intramural league. Its success led to a citywide program with more than 8,000 boys and girls taking part. The National Bowling Council provided financial support in 1945 to expand the program nationally and the following year it became the American Junior Bowling Congress.

The Young American Bowling Alliance, formed in 1982, was the result of combining three groups — the American Junior Bowling Congress, the Youth Bowling Association and ABC/WIBC Collegiate Division — into one.

USA Bowling

Founded as the United States Tenpin Bowling Federation in 1989 by ABC and WIBC, it became USA Bowling in 1993. One of USA Bowling's main duties was to select United States representatives for international competition.

It coordinated all amateur international competition promoted by the United States Olympic Committee or Federation Internationale des Quilleurs (FIQ, the world governing body for the sport) and conducted the USA Bowling National Amateur Championships. In addition, USA Bowling established instruction and coaching programs to help bowlers advance in ability.

United States Bowling Congress

On Jan. 1, 2005, ABC, WIBC, YABA and USA Bowling merged and became one organization, the United States Bowling Congress.

The national governing body for the sport of tenpin bowling in the United States, USBC now has the responsibility of maintaining uniform playing rules and equipment specifications standards for its nearly three million youth and adult members as the sport continues to evolve. (For more on USBC, see Chapter 15).

Certified Coaching Programs

USA Bowling and YABA administered programs to train and certify coaches to teach the sport of bowling. In May 2002, industry leaders voted to combine the two programs into one called USA Bowling Coaching.

USA Bowling Coaching became the USBC Coaching Program, which is the only coaching program for bowling recognized by the United States Olympic Committee.

1956 ABC Open Championships in Rochester, NY

THE PLAYING FIELD

Bowling Centers

Like any sport, bowling has its own unique places to play the game. They're called bowling centers and without them, there would be no bowling.

A modern bowling center offers more than just bowling with family and friends. Most bowling centers have a pro shop, restaurant and lounge, billiards and video games. Some might also offer outdoor activities such as golf, miniature golf, volleyball, batting cages and go-karts.

Centers can vary in size from two to 100 or more lanes and exist in settings such as tavern basements, large shopping complexes and casino hotels.

No matter the differences in size, location or style, all certified bowling centers feature lanes the same length and width, and pins with the same shape and weight. These centers are certified each year by the United States Bowling Congress as a service to its members. No other sport goes to such lengths to make sure all of its playing fields are certified.

Components of a Bowling Center

Although they vary in size, construction and services offered, all bowling centers have four common components:

Control Desk

The heart of most bowling centers is the control desk, where bowlers check in to receive a lane assignment, rental shoes (if they don't own their own) and get answers to the questions they might have about bowling or the bowling center.

Concourse

The concourse is the area behind the lanes and bowling area (Figure 2-1). This is where spectators gather and bowlers consume their food and drinks while bowling. Bowlers often change into and out of their bowling shoes and store their bowling bags in this area.

Figure 2-1, The Concourse, Bowling Area and Lanes

Bowling Area (settee)

The bowling area, or settee *(Figure 2-1)*, is the place where bowlers wait to bowl. A typical bowling area has a number of seats and a small scoring table.

IMPORTANT: Caring for a bowling center is everyone's responsibility. Bowlers should exercise good behavior and sportsmanship while bowling. Allowing food and drinks in the bowling area is not only a breach of good bowling etiquette but a safety issue, too. Bowlers should make it a point to leave food or drinks in the concourse area and to have their friends/team members do the same.

Lanes

Bowling takes place on the lanes. Lanes are described in detail in the next section of this chapter.

The Lane

It is important to note that all lanes are constructed within specifications provided by the United States Bowling Congress and must be maintained.

Lane Construction

Lanes are constructed either of wood or a synthetic material. Wooden lanes have 39 boards just over one-inch wide, each placed tightly side by side. Synthetic lanes have the same 39-board pattern laminated onto a synthetic surface. All lanes are 41½ to 42 inches wide from channel to channel, and 60 feet from the foul line to the head pin. With approximately another three feet from the head pin to the end the pin deck, the overall length is 63-3/16 feet. Bowling lanes have similar lane markings, with the exception of newer lanes that have added range finders at the end of the midlane(s).

Parts of a Lane

All bowlers should be familiar with the parts of a lane. When dealing with children, use simple descriptions; this will help them to understand the game to ensure they have fun. A bowling lane consists of these parts:
- Approach
- Foul line
- Front(s) (Heads)
- Midlane(s) (Pines)
- Backend(s)
- Pin deck
- Pin triangle
- Channels
- Boards

Approach

The approach *(Figure 2-2)* is a 15-16 foot (minimum specification is 15 feet) area where the bowler sets up and executes the delivery of the ball. The end of the approach is marked by the foul line, which separates the approach from the lane bed.

Three sets of locator dots *(Figure 2-2)* are positioned on the approach seven feet before the foul line.

The first two sets of dots are spaced 15 and 12 feet before the foul line. They are designed to help bowlers line up properly in their stance. Each locator dot in the two sets of dots is spaced five boards from the next dot and is positioned exactly in line with the dot in front of or behind it (To learn how to use these dots, refer to Chapter 5).

> NOTE: *Some approaches might only have five dots: two on either side of the large center dot, instead of three.*

The third set of dots is located just in front of the foul line. These dots are helpful in determining if a bowler has walked straight or at an angle to the lane (Refer to Chapter 8).

Each dot in the third set is exactly aligned with the corresponding dots in the first two sets.

Not only do the dots in all three sets line up with each other, they also line up with the corresponding target arrows on the lane.

Foul Line

The foul line *(Figure 2-2)* is a 3/8- to 1-inch boundary line that separates the approach from the rest of the lane. Just beyond the foul line is where the lane conditioner (oil) is applied. The oil is slippery and if the foul line is crossed, there is a risk of slipping and falling. If a bowler steps on or over the foul line or any other part of the bowler's person touches beyond the foul line, a foul is committed and they will receive a zero for that ball.

> NOTE: *The foul line comes into play only if the bowler releases the ball (known as a "legal delivery").*

Front(s)
(also known as heads)

The first 15 feet of the lane from the foul line to the target arrows is called the front(s) *(Figure 2-2)*. On wood lanes, the front(s) are traditionally made of hard maple wood to withstand the constant impact of bowling balls hitting the surface.

Midlane(s)
(also known as pines)

The next 30-foot section of the lane is referred to as the midlane(s) or pines *(Figure 2-2)*. On a wood lane, this section is constructed of soft pine wood. The midlane(s) takes far less punishment from bowling balls than the Front(s) because the ball normally never impacts the midlane(s) – it rolls on it. On wood lanes, the area where the hard maple wood of the Front(s) meets the soft wood of the pines is called a splice.

Figure 2-2

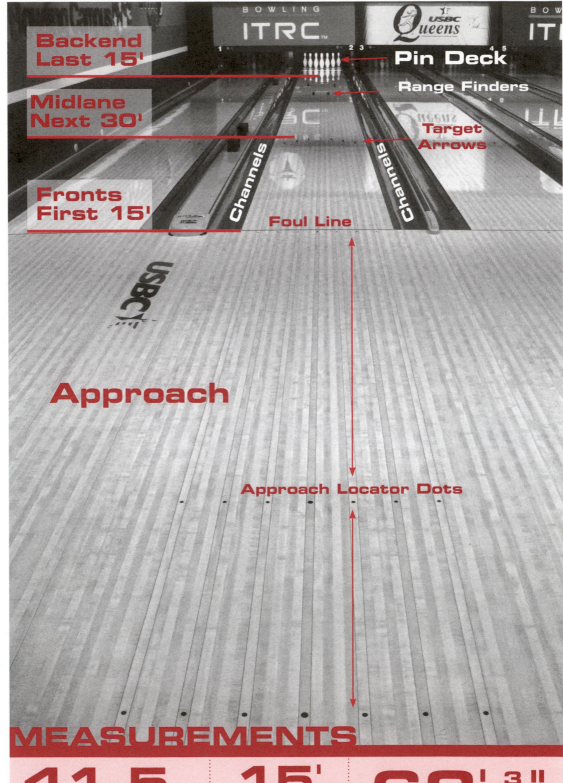

Backend Last 15'

Midlane Next 30'

Fronts First 15'

BOWLING **ITRC**™

Queens USBC

Pin Deck

Range Finders

Target Arrows

Channels

Channels

Foul Line

Approach

Approach Locator Dots

MEASUREMENTS

41.5 - .42"
Channel to Channel

.15' - 16'
from Approach to the foul line

63' $\frac{3}{16}$"
from pin deck to the foul line

Backend(s)

The last section of the lane is 15 feet. This area is known as the Backend(s) *(Figure 2-2)*. The Backend(s) of a wood lane is constructed of soft pine wood like the midlane(s). Generally, conditioner is not applied to this area as it allows the ball to encounter more friction with the lane surface, enabling the ball to hook.

Pin Deck

The pin deck *(Figure 2-7)* occupies the remaining four-foot area behind the Backend(s). It starts approximately one foot in front of the pins and includes a two-foot tail plank that protects the back edge from rebounding bowling balls. The pins are spotted in a triangular configuration. The pin deck on a wood lane is made of hard maple wood to withstand the impact of flying pins when struck by a bowling ball.

Channels

Two channels, one on each side of the lane *(Figure 2-2)*, run from the foul line to the end of the pin deck and represent an out-of-bounds area. The channel receives a ball that has been rolled off the lane and directs it past the pins to the end of the lane.

Boards

Bowling lane boards not only provide a specially-designed surface on which to bowl but also provide a built-in system for helping bowlers to properly align

themselves. For this system, one needs to know how the boards are numbered.

Boards are always numbered starting from the side where the bowler holds the ball. That is, a right-handed bowler will count from right to left with the Number 1 board starting next to the right channel then counting across the lane to the Number 39 board on the edge of the left channel. A left-handed bowler would count from left to right *(Figure 2-3)*. Either way, board Number 20 is in the middle of the lane for both right- and left-handed bowlers.

Lane Markings

All lanes are marked with target arrows and locator dots *(Figure 2-4)*. The arrows and dots are used in conjunction with the boards to help bowlers properly align their stance and aim. These arrows and dots have numbers *(Figure 2-3)*. For right-handed bowlers, the arrows and dots are numbered from right to left and for left-handed bowlers the arrows and dots are numbered from left to right.

Lane Locator Dots

The lane locator dots are positioned seven feet from the foul line on boards 3, 5, 8, 11 and 14 *(Figure 2-4)*. These dots are used to fine-tune a bowler's accuracy.

Target Arrows

There are seven target arrows located 15-17 feet from the foul line *(Figure 2-4)*. In relation to the boards, the

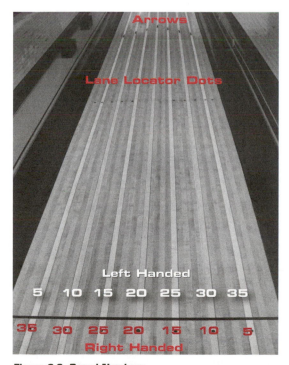

Figure 2-3, Board Numbers

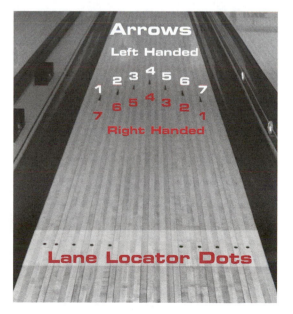

Figure 2-4, Lane Locator Dots and Arrows

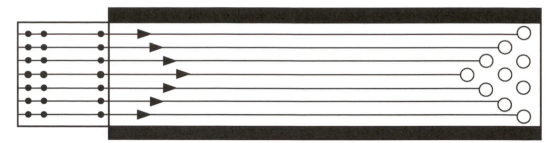

Figure 2-5, Dot-Arrow-Pin Alignment

target arrows are spaced every five boards from the middle board; therefore, the Number 4 target arrow is on board Number 20.

These target arrows aid bowlers in lining up for a shot. Even the youngest of bowlers should have a general understanding of how target arrows can help them get the ball where they want it to go on the lane.

Dot-Arrow-Pin Alignment

When standing at the back of the approach and looking down the lane, the three sets of locator dots on the approach and the arrows on the lane appear to be in dead-center alignment with the pins. In reality, this is true only for the large center dots, the fourth target arrow, and the one and/or five pin *(Figure 2-5)*.

Range Finders

At a point 33-44 feet beyond the foul line, there may be a maximum of four targets known as range finders *(Figure 2-6)*. Each target must be uniform in appearance and shall not be wider than a single board or longer than 36 inches. Range Fingers are located on the 10 and 15 boards on both sides of the lane. These help bowlers see the direction of the ball path farther down the lane.

The Pins

Pin Triangle

The 10 pins are arranged in a triangle in four rows on the pin deck, and are equally spaced 12 inches apart *(Figure 2-7)*.

Pins are numbered from 1 through 10. The 1-pin is called the head pin. Pins are numbered from left to right, front to back, so the two and three pins make up the second row, the 4, 5 and 6 pins comprise the third row, and the 7, 8, 9 and 10 pins are in the fourth row.

Pin construction
and regulations

Like lanes, pins are uniform in size, shape and weight. Each pin is 15 inches tall, approximately 4-11/16 inches in diameter and must weigh between three pounds, six ounces and three pounds, 10 ounces. Each individual lane must contain pins within this weight range. A pair of lanes must contain the same brand and model of pins with the same permit number.

Figure 2-6, Range Finders

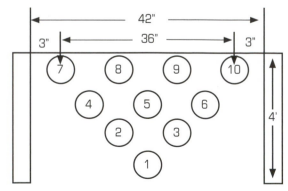

Figure 2-7, Pin Deck and Pin Arrangement

PERSONAL EQUIPMENT

Bowling Balls

Bowling Ball Basics

Bowling balls are drilled with holes for the thumb, the middle finger and the ring finger. The distance between the two finger holes and the thumb hole is known as the span; the distance between the two finger holes is known as the bridge *(Figure 3-1)*.

All bowling balls are 27 inches in circumference and approximately 8.5 inches in diameter. USBC regulations set the maximum weight of a bowling ball at 16 pounds. There is no minimum weight, but bowling balls lighter than six pounds are not manufactured.

The various markings on the outside of a bowling ball are the logo of the manufacturer, the brand name of the ball and a serial number.

Selecting the Right House Ball

Choosing the proper bowling ball is important for bowlers. Most bowling centers have a large selection of bowling balls of varying weights and hole sizes that are available for customers. These "house balls" usually have the weight marked on the ball.

House balls are sized to accommodate a large group of customers. Though they will rarely be a perfect fit, it is important to find one that fits best.

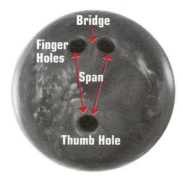

Figure 3-1, Bowling Ball Holes, Span and Bridge

There are four factors to consider when selecting the correct bowling ball:
Weight
Grip types
Span
Hole sizes

Weight

The ball should be the correct weight, meaning that it is heavy enough to use without overpowering the bowler. As a starting point, youth bowlers should select a ball that is about 10 percent of their body weight. Younger bowlers may opt to use a two-handed delivery or two-handed approach (See Chapter 14).

For adults, general guidelines are 12 to 14 pound balls for women and 14 to 16 pounds for men.

Most beginners tend to choose a ball that is too light, leading to problems with their swing. Bowlers should not be afraid of trying a heavier ball.

Weight Selection Techniques

Use one of the following procedures to fine-tune the selection process:
Palm test
1. Hold the bowling hand waist-high, palm up and out in front.
2. Place a bowling ball into the palm.
3. Look for a ball weight that moves the hand slightly downward.

Ball sling
Another technique in determining proper ball weight is to use a ball sling. A ball sling is a piece of cloth with two handles that bowlers use to carry a ball.

Place the ball inside the sling and use the thumb and two bowling fingers to hold the handle.

Gently swing the ball backward and forward as if bowling.

Look for a fairly free armswing where the bowler cannot easily change the direction of the swing plane. It should not be so heavy that it physically alters the bowler's posture and balance.

Grip test

The grip test determines whether a bowler can hold the ball hanging at their side with one hand for 10 to 15 seconds without visible discomfort or struggling to maintain the grip.

Grip Types

There are two basic types of grips in bowling: conventional and fingertip.

Conventional: Beginning bowlers should start using a conventional grip. This means that the middle and ring fingers are inserted to the second joint, with the thumb fully inserted. The conventional grip can give the bowler a sense of secure grip when swinging the ball. This is why most house balls are drilled with a conventional grip.

Fingertip: With a fingertip grip, the middle and ring fingers enter to the first joint, with the thumb fully inserted. Once mastering the basic techniques of the sport, it is recommended to advance to the fingertip grip. This grip, which is used by most experienced bowlers, encourages a quicker and smoother release which allows the bowler to hook the ball easier.

Figure 3-2, Checking the span Conventional (l) and Fingertip Grip (r)

Span

The distance between the thumb and finger holes is known as the span *(Figure 3-1)*. The span must fit the hand size. A "quick check" for proper conventional grip span is to insert the thumb in the ball and then lay the fingers over the holes *(Figure 3-2)*. The span is correct when the second joint of the middle two fingers is half way between the front edge and back edge of the holes.

Hole Size

The fingers should fit comfortably snug. After inserting the fingers into the ball, the thumb should be able to be inserted entirely into the ball. A correct-fitting thumb hole is just big enough to allow the thumb to come out of the ball easily. With the thumb inserted fully, it will allow the bowler to swing the ball freely.

Personal Bowling Balls

While using house balls is a fine temporary option, many bowlers choose to purchase their own ball that

is drilled specifically for their bowling hand. It is recommended to have balls drilled by an International Bowling Pro Shop and Instructors Association (IBPSIA) professional. Balls can be plugged (filled with a special compound) and re-drilled a couple of times before a new one is needed.

Purchasing a ball is recommended simply to ensure that it is of consistent weight and a proper fit. In terms of improved performance and safety, it will be one of the wisest investments a bowler can make.

Parts of a Bowling Ball

A bowling ball is composed of two major components: the outside known as the shell or coverstock, and the inside which is the weight block.

The coverstock is made of a durable material, which can withstand the impact of the ball landing on the lane and hitting the pins. Coverstocks can be sanded or polished to create early or later hook on the lane (see altering the surface later in this chapter).

The internal weight block is usually constructed of heavy, dense materials. The original purpose was to help maintain the balance and weight of the ball after the holes were drilled, but today's weight blocks help add to the dynamics of the bowling ball. The shape of the weight block along with how it is positioned when being drilled can create a specific reaction on the lane. Weight blocks vary in size, weights and shapes depending on the equipment manufacturer. Bowlers should consult a USBC certified coach and an IBPSIA professional to help with equipment selection.

Cover stocks

The most important consideration when selecting a ball is the outside shell or coverstock. On the lane, balls with different types of coverstocks will react differently. Some coverstocks are more aggressive, creating more friction with the surface of the lane thus providing earlier traction and potentially earlier hook. Less aggressive coverstocks create less friction with the lane surface providing more skid and potentially later hook. Note: Bowlers must provide a degree of side rotation in order for a ball to hook.

In today's game, there are four distinct coverstock types being used:
• Plastic (polyester)
• Urethane
• Resin
• Particle

Plastic: Plastic balls have a very smooth surface and will generally go straight. This type of ball is recommended for beginning bowlers.

Urethane: Urethane balls are more porous and will generate some hook. This type of ball is recommended for bowlers who are looking for more overall hook but with a controllable reaction.

Resin: Resin balls have a tacky surface and have the ability to hook more aggressively. These balls are recommended for the intermediate to advanced players.

Particle: Particle balls are very aggressive; they have microscopic particles imbedded into the surface and are best suited when the lanes have more lane conditioner/oil than normal. Intermediate or advanced players may benefit from using particle balls as well.

Altering the Surface of Personal Equipment

Changing the surface texture of a bowling ball will alter the path the ball travels down a lane by affecting when, where and how much a ball will hook on a lane. A ball that has a rough (sanded) surface will create the potential for the ball to react, or hook, earlier on the lane. A ball with a smooth (polished) surface will result in the ball reacting later on the lane.

It is recommended that surface alterations be performed by an IBPSIA professional. In USBC certified events, changing a bowling ball's surface is only allowed prior to the start of competition.

Sanding

Advanced bowlers will sometimes use abrasives such as sandpaper, Scotchbrite™ or Abralon™ pads to alter the surface of their bowling balls. They do this to make the surface rougher, which will make the ball hook earlier. Sanding creates grooves on the surface which gives the oil a place to go, just like a snow tire with deep treads.

The oil will seep into the grooves, allowing the peaks on the surface to stay in contact with the lane, creating more friction and greater potential for ball reaction.

Polishing

Polishing the ball's surface will have the opposite effect of sanding. Polishing fills the grooves on the ball, making the surface smooth and decreasing the friction between the ball and the lane. This action will cause the ball to skid further and hook later, at times with a sharper angle of entry to the pins.

Keeping Your Ball Clean

Simply keeping the surface of your bowling ball clean is important. The conditioner/oil picked up from the lane will build up and soak into the ball's surface, which will delay and reduce the amount of hook. Cleaning products are available in pro shops that will remove oil from the coverstock to help maintain a consistent reaction.

A list of approved ball cleaners is available on BOWL.com.

Figure 3-3, Rental Shoes
· · · · · · · · · · · · · · · · · · ·

Bowling Shoes

Special bowling shoes made with leather or synthetic soles allow the bowler to slide as the ball is being delivered. Shoes may be either rented at the center or purchased from a pro shop.

Rental shoes *(Figure 3-3)*, available at the control desk, will have leather soles on both the right and left shoes. Because rental shoes are constructed with leather/synthetic soles on both shoes, it allows right- or left-handed bowlers to use them.

Bowlers may choose to purchase shoes. A pair of inexpensive personal bowling shoes will be constructed similar to rental shoes, with slide soles on both shoes, while a more expensive, high-performance shoe is constructed with two different soles: leather/synthetic for the sliding foot and rubber on the other foot. The rubber-soled shoe will provide necessary traction prior to the last step when delivering the ball. Right-handed bowlers will have the traction shoe on the right foot and left-handed bowlers will have the traction shoe on the left foot (Caution: If the bowler slides with their ball-side foot, the traction sole needs to be on the opposite foot).

Proper Clothing

It is important to wear comfortable-fitting clothing when bowling but not so loose that it will get in the way of maintaining a fluid movement. Freedom of movement across the shoulders and under the arms is imperative, as is the ability to bend at the knee with no restriction.

MODERN RULES OF BOWLING

History and Formation of Modern Rules

There were several attempts at creating a national governing body for the sport of tenpin bowling but none were successful until the American Bowling Congress was founded in 1895.

Preceding the ABC, delegates from nine bowling clubs met in New York in 1875 and organized the National Bowling Association. This first attempt to bring order from chaos is still evident as some agreed upon legislation still is in effect.

While gambling continued to be a problem in some areas, the lack of uniform playing rules and equipment specifications limited the development of the game until the ABC was formed on Sept. 9, 1895 in New York City. With the formation of the ABC, many of the disagreements between bowling clubs were settled. As the sport's governing body, ABC's regulations served as the road map for which all future organizations would fashion their regulations.

There have been a number of rules modifications over the years, but no significant alterations in equipment specifications. Equipment specifications changes have

1905 ABC Tournament held in Milwaukee

been adopted to meet the changes brought on by such technological advancements as automation and the invention of plastic, nylon and other synthetics. These changes occur today as necessary.

Modern Rules

Let's review some basic rules of bowling:
• The foul line
• Scoring
• Pinfall

The Foul Line

The foul line should be viewed as "out of bounds" in bowling. If the foul line is crossed with any part of the body (footwear and clothing included) and come in contact with the lane after releasing the ball, it is a foul and the resulting pinfall is zero for that turn.

The 42-inch long black line that separates the approach from the lane is not the only part of the foul line. The foul line runs the entire length of the bowling center. If a bowler delivered a shot on Lane 3, then ran down and put their hand on the wall past the foul line, it would be considered a foul.

A foul can occur any time during a delivery; until the next bowler steps onto the approach to prepare to bowl, it is still considered the previous bowler's turn, and will be called a foul if that bowler touches or crosses the foul line.

If a bowler touches or crosses the foul line without releasing the ball, it is not a foul and they can go back and start again.

Most bowling centers have "foul lights" that will trip a buzzer if a bowler fouls. However, if that light does not work or is not turned on, it still is a foul if the line is crossed.

Crossing the foul line also can be very dangerous as it is easy to slip and fall on the conditioner applied to the lane.

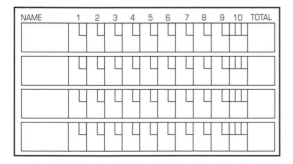

Figure 4-1, Sample Scorecard

Scoring

Scoring in bowling is quite basic though it appears complex. A game consists of 10 frames. A bowler gets two chances in each frame to knock down pins *(Figure 4-1)*.

To score the game of bowling, bowlers need to understand that the final score in a frame does not always reflect actual pins knocked down. The score can also include a series of "bonus" pins.

Look at scoring this way:

A **strike** (when all the pins are knocked down on the first attempt) is worth 10 points plus the number of pins knocked down with the next two shots.

A **spare** (when the remaining pins are knocked down on the second attempt) is worth 10 points plus the number of pins knocked down with the next shot.

An **open** frame (when pins are left standing after two shots) is worth the number of pins knocked down in that frame.

A **split** is a spare leave in which the head pin is down and two or more pins remain standing, with the intermediate pins knocked down in front and in between.

A **foul** occurs when a part of the bowler's body touches or goes beyond the foul line. The bowler receives zero for that delivery. Any pins knocked down are reset if the foul occurs on the first delivery.

Looking at this concept further, a game of bowling can be broken down into five basic results: Strike, spare, open, split and foul.

A strike is perfection. When a bowler strikes, the score is not actually added up until the next two shots are rolled. Let's say a bowler rolled a strike and on the next ball in the next frame they get eight and then they knock down one pin on the following shot. The bowler would add 19 to the frame in which they scored a strike (10 for the strike + 8 + 1 = 19 *(Figure 4-2)*.

If the bowler scored a strike and then strikes in the next two frames, they add 30 to the frame in which they scored the first strike and add bonus points until the bowler stops striking.

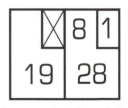

Figure 4-2, Scoring a strike

The perfect game: 300

If a bowler rolls 12 consecutive strikes in one game, they have achieved a 300, the highest score attainable in bowling *(Figure 4-3)*

A spare is scored similar to a strike. Say the bowler rolls the ball and knocks down eight pins; they mark eight on the scoresheet and roll the next shot. If the remaining

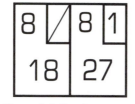

1	2	3	4	5	6	7	8	9	10
☒	☒	☒	☒	☒	☒	☒	☒	☒	☒☒☒
30	60	90	120	150	180	210	240	270	300

Figure 4-3, Perfect Game

two pins are knocked down, the bowler records a spare. Now, they get eight on the first ball of the next frame so they enter a score of 18 in the frame where the spare was scored (10 for the spare + 8 = 18). On the second roll then knock down one more pin, now they add nine to the score for a running total of 27 *(Figure 4-4)*.

An open frame occurs when there are pins standing after two shots have been rolled. This means that the bowler didn't get a spare or strike, and the frame is open. For example, the bowler knocks down eight

Figure 4-4, Scoring a spare

pins with the first roll, and gets neither of the remaining pins with the next shot. They receive the total of the pins knocked down, eight, and no bonus points and add it to their score *(Figure 4-4 and 4-5)*.

A split is simply a difficult spare leave. The distinction between a split and a spare is that the pins left standing on the first shot stand in such a way that it is difficult to knock them down. For example, the 7-10 split is virtually impossible to pick up because the two pins are on opposite sides of the lane.

Figure 4-5, Scoring an Open Frame

Whether the shot is a split or not has nothing to do with how the score is added. If the split is converted, a spare will marked and bonus pins awarded. If the split is not picked up, it's considered an open frame. A split is usually noted on the scoresheet or screen by circling the number of pins that were knocked down on the first shot.

Bowlers should understand how a foul affects their score. If they foul on the first shot of the frame, they receive zero for that attempt with the chance for a second delivery (the pins are reset to a full rack of 10). If they knock down all 10 pins on the second delivery, the result is a spare for the frame. If they foul while attempting to complete a spare, a zero is received for that delivery as well, and the score will be zero for that frame.

The 10th frame is treated differently because bowlers have the opportunity to make it a "bonus" frame *(Figure*

4-6). A bowler will receive two bonus shots if they start the frame with a strike. The bowler receives one bonus shot if they start the frame by converting a spare.

The fewest possible shots a bowler could throw in a game of bowling is 11 (strikes in the first nine frames with an open in the 10th frame). The most shots a bowler can throw in one game is 21 (two shots per frame with a spare in the 10th and a bonus ball).

Pinfall

Pinfall in bowling is what it's all about. However, there are distinctions between legal and illegal pinfall.

Legal pinfall results when the ball hits the pins and knocks them over, either by contact with the ball or from other pins that have been knocked over by the shot.

Illegal pinfall results when the delivery counts but the resulting pinfall does not. If the bowler is entitled to another delivery, the pins must be respotted before the bowler continues. Examples include:

- The ball leaves the lane before reaching the pins or the ball bounces out of the channel and knocks over pins.
- The ball rebounds from the rear cushion and knocks over pins.
- A mechanical – or human – pinsetter touches the pins.
- A foul is committed.
- A bowler rolls the shot when there are pins in the channel or on the lane from a previous shot, and the ball touches those pins. These pins are called "dead wood" since they are not in play.

A dead ball is another instance in which a delivery does not legally count. When a dead ball is called, the delivery does not count and the correct pins must be respotted. The bowler is allowed to rebowl that delivery. Among the situations when a dead ball would be called include:

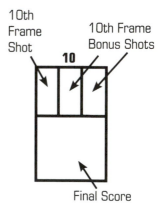

Figure 4-6, 10th Frame

- Any bowler calls attention to the fact that one or more pins were missing from the setup after a delivery.
- A bowler bowls on the wrong lane or out of turn.
- A delivered ball contacts a foreign object on the lane.
- Any pin is moved or knocked down as a bowler delivers the ball but before the ball reaches the pins.

Types of Bowling

There are three general ways to play the sport of bowling:
- Open play
- League
- Tournament

Open Play

Open play consists of a variety of organized or unorganized options.

Unorganized open play can be friends getting together, youth bowling with their parents or a couple out on a date. It also can be someone practicing on their game with a coach.

Organized open play features activities such as birthday parties, company outings or "glow bowling".

League

League bowling has been the backbone of the sport since the ABC was born. People form teams from one to five players (based on the league rules) and compete on a regular basis (weekly, bi-weekly or monthly) for a specific number of games. Traditionally, league coordinators create competitive league schedules. At the end of the league season, a team will win and be acknowledged as the champions.

USBC certifies leagues at thousands of bowling centers in the United States, which insures an organized structure, approved rules, awards and other benefits.

Because of the handicap system created and encouraged by USBC, new bowlers can compete successfully in most USBC leagues. Handicap bowling leagues exist so that bowlers with a variety of averages can be in a league together and compete equally.

For bowlers interested in finding a certified league in their area, they should go to their local bowling center and talk to someone at the control counter. Most bowling centers have a league coordinator and or sign-up sheets. Bowlers let the bowling center personnel know their skill level (beginner, intermediate or advanced) and they are placed in a league that will best suit their needs.

Fall and/or winter leagues usually start around Labor Day and can last from eight to 36 weeks; however, leagues start at other times of the year as well. There are numerous types of leagues, so a bowler should be able to find one that suits their needs.

Types of leagues include handicap, scratch, mixed, gender specific, youth, adult/youth, senior, traveling, company, special interest, school and Sport.

Bowlers should choose a league with people that share their skill level and have similar interests so they will be more likely to enjoy the experience.

Each league has a secretary who takes care of scheduling weekly team competition and lane assignments, calculating averages and handicaps, and posting the standings and other statistics. This information is generally posted in the bowling center or may be found on BOWL.com.

Basic League Rules

Keep in mind that every USBC league should adhere to two sets of rules – USBC playing rules and the league rules. League rules are specific to each league, yet fall into the parameters established by USBC. At the yearly league meeting, rules should be discussed and voted on.

People join leagues to compete, have fun and socialize. People might think that mixing too many rules with a night out for some friendly competition will get in the way of having fun, but paying attention to the league's structure, format and rules allows for a more enjoyable night of bowling.

Let's look at some basic league rules and concepts including: alternate lane bowling, teams and schedules, averages, handicap, points and standings, absent (blind) and vacancy scores.

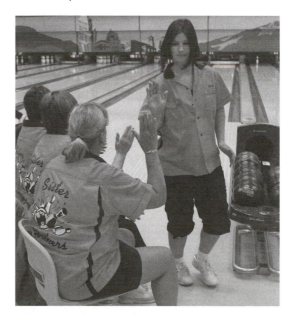

League bowling has long been the backbone of the sport. The USBC offers bowlers a wide variety of league bowling options.

Alternate lane bowling

When bowling in a league, teams will alternate lanes on the assigned pair. For example, if Team A starts on Lane 1, each team member will bowl in a specified order and then move to Lane 2 for the second frame of bowling, following Team B. After Team A has finished its order on Lane 2, they will return to Lane 1 for the third frame and continue in order from there.

Be aware that once a team starts bowling, the order must remain the same. The team may start on the alternate lane once the other team has finished, but it is recommended to bowl at the same pace as the other team.

Alternate lane bowling makes competition fair for all players because everyone competes on both lanes. If a team bowled exclusively on one lane that scored easier, they would have an unfair advantage.

Teams and Schedules

To be considered a USBC certified league, it must have a minimum of four teams.

Each team has a captain, who is the team representative and performs various duties including: determining a roster of eligible players, collecting league fees and USBC membership dues, being responsible for team conduct, entering the team lineup, signing scoresheets and awarding prize money received at the end of the season.

USBC provides standard schedules for leagues to follow. Leagues can be divided in halves, thirds or quarters, with winners of each segment competing in playoffs to determine the league champion.

It's this type of competition, along with social interaction, that keeps a league interesting.

Averages

The term "average" in a bowling league is an average score that represents a bowler's skill level. To calculate an average, divide the total number of pins by the number of games bowled. For example, if a bowler has completed nine games and has a total pinfall of 1,354, then the average would be 150 (1,354 divided by 9 = 150.4; fractions are disregarded). If bowling in more than one league, a separate average for each league will be established.

Handicap

A bowler's handicap is based on the person's league average. Handicap helps level the playing field since a bowler with a 180 average would win almost every time if bowling against someone with a 140 average. Handicap gives bowlers additional pins to add to their score so different skill levels can compete equally.

Handicap is calculated from a base average, usually between 70 and 100 percent. A bowler's average is subtracted from that base then multiplied by the percentage chosen. Example: Bowler "A" has a 180 average. If the base is 210 and handicap used is 80 percent, then subtract 180 from 210 then multiply the difference by 80 percent to produce a 24-pin handicap (210-180=30; 30x.80=24). Adding the 24 pins to the 180 average produces a handicap average of 204 (180+24=204).

USBC recommends higher handicap percentages for more equalized matches.

Handicap can be based on an individual format or a team format. The team format adds the averages of all players and handicap is based off that total.

Example of team handicap: A five-player team uses handicap based on 200 per player. The averages of the "Why Not Us?" team are: 145, 162, 131, 195 and 210. To get the team handicap (based on 100 percent of 1,000 for the team) all the players' averages are added up which total 843. The team subtracts 843 from 1,000, which equals 157. The team will receive 157 pins handicap for each game.

Handicapping procedures and examples are listed in the USBC Rulebook.

Scratch

Scratch bowling leagues compete using the actual score, which means bowlers do not receive a handicap adjustment to their score.

Though scratch leagues are normally comprised of experienced or high-average players, there are scratch leagues where individuals or teams cannot exceed a certain average. For instance, a bowler could find a scratch league where the averages must be 180 or below.

Some leagues put a cap on a team's entering average. For example, a league might cap a five-player team's entering average at 1,000 so teams would have to put together their team using bowlers with averages that do not exceed that 1,000 cap. This cap can change depending on how many players constitute a team and what the league chooses to vote on. The bottom line is a scratch league can be formed to accommodate all types of skill levels.

Points and Standings

Standing sheets are used to keep track of points awarded in league. A typical league session consists of teams bowling three games. For example, in a seven-point system, two points are awarded for each game and one point is awarded to the team with the highest total pinfall (series) for the session.

There are many point systems used in leagues. Some award individual points in addition to team points. In this system, bowlers earn points for beating the opposing team's bowler in the same lineup position. Example, the lead-off bowler scores higher than the other team's lead-off bowler, they win the point(s) which is added to the team points. This system can be used in handicap or scratch leagues.

Opening shots at the 2009 USBC Open Championships in Las Vegas.

Standing sheets are available for bowlers each time the league bowls. They show ranking of teams by points based on wins and losses, and individual statistics and averages along with the season's highest scores.

Absentee and vacancy scores

Absentee/blind and vacancy scores are used when teams do not have a full team. The absentee/blind or vacancy score is determined by league rules but typically is calculated by subtracting 10 pins from the absent/blind bowler's average including individual handicap.

A vacancy score is usually 120 plus handicap, unless the league votes to use another score.

Traveling

Traveling leagues compete at two or more bowling centers, alternating weeks.

Sport Bowling

USBC Sport Bowling leagues are available to youth and adult USBC members who join the Sport Bowling program for an additional membership fee.

Sport leagues are conducted on more challenging lane conditions than a standard league (see Chapter 9).

The possibilities for league bowling are endless and make for interesting competition. The bowling center's top priority is to provide everyone an opportunity to enjoy the lifelong sport.

Tournaments

Tournaments are events that can take place over one day, one weekend, or several months where prize money, trophies, medals, and scholarships can be won. Tournament competition ranges from local, state and national championships to international events where countries compete for medals. Tournaments are available for every skill level and are a great opportunity for the competitive bowler whether they are handicap or scratch.

There are several types of tournaments:

Championship Events

USBC members have the opportunity to test their skills in a competitive environment by participating in certified championship tournaments. Bowlers are assigned to compete in different divisions based on their average.

In most championship tournaments, bowlers may enter multiple events. The most common events are team (four- or five-person), doubles and singles, and all-events. A bowler's all-events score is comprised of the total pinfall of all games bowled.

This format is used by the largest bowling tournaments in the world, including the USBC Open Championships, USBC Women's Championships and the USBC Youth Open. These tournaments are held in different cities of the United States each year.

Baker Format

The Baker System is a format that calls for different players on a team to bowl in different frames. For example, bowler number 1 in the lineup throws in the first and sixth frames; bowler number 2 throws in the second and seventh frames, etc. The format is named after Frank K. Baker, former executive secretary-treasurer of the American Bowling Congress.

Elimination

Some tournaments use a format that calls for entrants to bowl a specified number of qualifying games before a pre-determined number of players are eliminated.

USBC Annual Tournaments

The USBC administers a variety of annual tournaments for its members that offer a wonderful way to experience all that is great about bowling: friendship, competition and fun on the lanes. A brief look at each of these events:

1. USBC Open Championships

The USBC Open Championships (formerly the ABC Championships Tournament) is the world's largest participatory sporting event. It consists of team, doubles and singles competition, plus optional all-events.

The event, which attracts 60,000 to 90,000 participants annually, is open to all USBC adult members (except PBA Tour professionals) who compete for millions of dollars in prize money. The Championships feature two average-based divisions and are conducted in an arena or convention center setting, allowing USBC members to experience competition in a stadium-like atmosphere.

2. USBC Women's Championships

The USBC Women's Championships (formerly the WIBC Championship Tournament) is the world's largest bowling tournament for women. The annual tournament attracts tens of thousands of women bowlers from every U.S. state as well as international participants who compete for millions of dollars in prize money. Women of all ages and levels of ability compete in three average-based divisions.

3. USBC Team USA Trials

The USBC Team USA Trials is used to determine who becomes a member of Team USA and Junior Team USA, the teams that represent the United States in international competition. The adult team is selected

from the participants at the USBC Team USA Trials; the youth team is selected at the USBC Junior Gold Championships and the USBC Team USA Trials.

4. USBC Intercollegiate Team Championships

The USBC Intercollegiate Team Championships (formerly the Intercollegiate Bowling Championships) is the pinnacle event of the college bowling season. This tournament brings together the country's top men's and women's teams to compete for national titles. Teams advance to this tournament through sectional competitions.

5. USBC Intercollegiate Singles Championships

The USBC Intercollegiate Singles Championships (formerly the Collegiate Singles Championships) features the top male and female collegiate bowlers in the country competing for individual national titles. Qualifying for the national finals is held at USBC Intercollegiate Team Championships sectional qualifier sites.

6. USBC Masters

The USBC Masters (formerly the ABC Masters) is one of professional bowling's most prestigious events and one of the four majors on the Professional Bowlers Association Tour. USBC members who meet a minimum average requirement (190 as of 2005) are eligible to compete in the Masters.

7. USBC Senior Masters

The USBC Senior Masters (formerly the ABC Senior Masters) features some of the sport's top professional and amateur senior players. USBC members who are at least 50 years old and meet a minimum average requirement (190 as of 2005) are eligible to compete in the Senior Masters.

8. USBC Queens and Senior Queens

The prestigious USBC Queens (formerly the WIBC Queens) attracts high-average amateur and professional women bowlers. The USBC Senior Queens (formerly the WIBC Senior Queens) attracts high-average amateur and professional women bowlers age 50 and over. The USBC Queens, USBC Senior Queens and the USBC Women's Championships are held simultaneously in the same host city.

9. USBC Senior Championships

Senior bowlers can qualify for the USBC Senior Championships (formerly the ABC/WIBC Senior Championships) by entering their state association senior tournaments. To advance to the national level

2010 USBC Queens winner Kelly Kulick

of the Senior Championships, a bowler must have won the all-events portion in their respective age division at their state association senior tournament.

10. USBC Junior Gold Championships

The USBC Junior Gold Championships features the best North American and international youth bowlers competing for college scholarships, individual national titles and berths on Junior Team USA. USBC Junior Gold members advance to the USBC Junior Gold Championships through qualifying events held across the country. The tournament awards upward of $140,000 in scholarships each year.

11. Pepsi USBC Youth Championships

The Pepsi USBC Youth Championships begins with league level qualifying and has six divisions. Winners in each division will advance to the state/zone competition with some earning scholarships. The winners and runners-up of the Scratch Divisions from the state/zone finals will receive a berth from USBC into the USBC Junior Gold Championships.

12. USBC Youth Open

USBC Youth Open participants get the chance to compete against other bowlers from across the country and around the world. Bowlers are separated into four divisions based on average and compete in singles and doubles, team, and all-events. Each year, approximately 3,000 youth bowlers gather in a host city with the chance to win their share of more than $100,000 in scholarship money.

Information about these events can be found on the USBC website, BOWL.com, or by calling (800) 514-BOWL.

Bowling Etiquette

When people go bowling, they expect to have a good time. That means enjoying time with family and friends, relaxing in the pleasant atmosphere of the bowling center and getting some good exercise while developing skills.

Knowing the proper etiquette will make the experience on the lanes more fun for everyone.

Lane Courtesy

Lane courtesy is a time-honored tradition in bowling. If a bowler is on the approach, the person on the lane next to them waits until that bowler has started their delivery before stepping onto the approach. Respect works both ways.

Who Bowls First?

When there are two people on the approach at the same time, who should bowl first? The general rule: the first one up should go. If there is any question who was the first one there, the person to the right, or on the higher numbered lane, has the right of way.

Don't Wait: Just Do It!

Once a bowler is lined up in their stance, they shouldn't wait. The time for thinking about a shot is before the bowler gets in the stance. Once they step onto the approach, the time for thinking is over. Just do it! After the shot is made, the bowler should hold a balanced finish position until the ball hits the pins and then return to the bowlers' area.

Adopting these guidelines helps promote a well-paced game and a more enjoyable experience for everyone.

Practice Restraint

In the heat of competition, emotions and enthusiasm run high. That's one reason bowling is such a great sport.

Just make sure enthusiasm doesn't hinder or irritate other bowlers.

Bowling is a wholesome family sport; refrain from using profanity in the bowling center.

A negative mental attitude, temper tantrum, kicking the ball return, scoring table or other equipment is inexcusable. It will do more than just aggravate teammates, it will affect personal performance.

Caring for a bowling center is everyone's responsibility; remember, the condition of a center reflects on the public's perception of bowlers, and bowling as a sport.

PREPARING TO BOWL AND THE STANCE

When bowlers enter the bowlers' area, they should check for safety issues. The most common issue is finding something on the floor that will cause problems if it gets onto the bottom of bowling shoes. Spills and other liquids will cause shoes to stick on the approach. Powder, dust and other substances may cause shoes to become slippery.

These same problems can occur on the approach. Bowlers should take a test slide at the foul line without the ball to determine the condition of the approach.

Problems that can happen to bowling shoes:

On rainy or snowy days, moisture can be tracked in.

Food and beverages can be spilled.

Water on the floor in restrooms.

Dynamic and Static Stretching Exercises

Bowling injuries, such as sore muscles and sprains, may be significantly reduced by properly warming up. While some injuries are caused by accidents, others are the result of strain and stress on the body that builds up over time. In bowling, these injuries build up in the shoulder, back, elbow, wrist, hand, knees and legs. This is most often seen as soreness or stiffness in the hours or days after bowling.

The principal cause of these injuries is lack of pre-bowling warm-up. Performing simple warm-up exercises before bowling will loosen muscles and joints, prepare the body for maximum physical performance and help prevent injury.

The following warm-up exercises are designed to specifically loosen those muscles used the most during bowling. Bowlers should perform 5-10 minutes of light cardio such as jogging or jumping jacks followed by 30 seconds of the following dynamic stretching exercises. (These exercises are most effective when they are performed once or twice daily and especially just before bowling).

Dynamic Stretches

Arm Circles: Extend arms out to the side while standing straight (wing span), then start rotating arms in small circles and increase in size. Do forward and backward *(Figure 5-1)*.

Walking Toe Touches: Kick leg forward as high as possible without causing pain; looks like a toy soldier *(Figure 5-2)*.

Walking Lunges with Trunk Rotations: Forward lunge and in the down position rotate body to the left and right *(Figure 5-3)*.

Windmills: Arms extended out to the side while standing straight (wing span) and legs slightly apart, bend over at waist and then rotate trunk – right hand to left foot, then left hand to right foot *(Figure 5-4)*.

Iron Crosses: Lying on back with arms out from the body. Lift right leg up and rotate over toward left hand. Try and get the foot as close to the hand without raising the shoulders off the floor. Repeat with left leg *(Figure 5-5)*.

Scorpions: Similar to Iron Crosses except lying on stomach. Lift leg up and rotate back toward opposite hand *(Figure 5-6)*.

Chain Breakers: With arms extended out to the side while standing straight (wing span), bring arms across body and then back out *(Figure 5-7)*.

Figure 5-1, Arm Circles

Figure 5-2

Figure 5-3

Figure 5-4

Figure 5-5

Figure 5-6

Figure 5-7

Some of the Dynamic stretches shown above

Static Stretches

The following static stretching exercises provide the best results when performed after bowling. These exercises performed with long, slow breaths will relax and cool down the muscles, aiding in the limitation of muscle soreness.

Wrist Flexors: Extend arm with palm facing out and hand bent up at the wrist. Grasp fingers with other hand. Pull toward body. Repeat with other hand.

Wrist Extenders: Extend arm with hand bent downward at the wrist. Grasp fingers with other hand. Pull toward body. Repeat with other hand.

Triceps: Lift elbow of one arm over head (with elbow bent so the hand is behind the back. Grasp elbow with opposite hand and pull gently toward middle of head, alternate with the other arm.

Quadriceps: Balance on one leg while grasping the foot of the other leg and stretch it back to the opposite buttock. Alternate with the other leg. This will stretch the front leg muscles. Be sure to hold onto something for support during this exercise.

Side Stretch: Extend right arm over head while keeping other arm at side. Bend sideways at the waist toward left side. Alternate with other side.

Hip Flexor Stretch: Place left leg in back and right leg in front of the body. By bending the right knee and extending the left leg, shift weight forward and hold. Alternate leg position and repeat.

Calf Stretch version 1: Balance balls of feet on a small stair (such as the approach), then lower and raise body at the ankle.

Calf Stretch version 2: Place palms up against a wall. Place left leg in back and right leg in front of the body. Stretch out left leg by bending right knee until tension is felt and hold. Repeat with legs alternated.

Bowling Ball Safety

A bowling ball is a slick, smooth, heavy object that can easily slip from a bowler's grasp. Before a bowler picks up a bowling ball, they should dry their hands with a towel or use the air blower located on the ball return.

When a bowler picks up a ball from the return, they should grasp it on the sides using both hands. This prevents them from getting their fingers hurt from another ball rolling into them *(Figure 5-8)*. After the ball has been picked up, it is cradled in the opposite arm. This helps the bowling hand conserve strength for the delivery.

If a bowler is lifting someone else's bowling bag, they should be careful as they do not know the weight. Many bowlers carry two or more bowling balls in each bag. With the addition of shoes, wrist aids and other accessories the combined weight can be more than 50

Figure 5-8, Correct/incorrect ways of picking up ball

Figure 5-10, Starting positions for left handed (left) and for right handed (right)

pounds. When bowlers lift equipment in and out of the vehicle, they should keep their back muscles straight and use leg muscles to lift.

Inserting Hand

When a bowler is in position and ready to put their hand into the ball, they will insert their middle and ring fingers first. For a conventional grip, they should be inserted to the second joint; for a fingertip grip, insert the fingers to the first joint. Once the fingers are set into a comfortable position, the bowler should insert the thumb all the way (Refer to Chapter 3).

Starting Position on the Approach

Determining where a bowler stands on the approach is important for consistency. This allows them to have a reference point from which adjustments can be made. There are two considerations in figuring out where to stand; first, is how far from the foul line should the bowler stand and, second, should they stand on the left or right side of the approach.

Distance from the Foul Line

To find a starting point, a bowler should go to the foul line, face the bowlers' area and place the back of their heels within two inches of the foul line. They will take 4-1/2 brisk walking steps while looking straight ahead then pivot on their toe and face the pins. This is

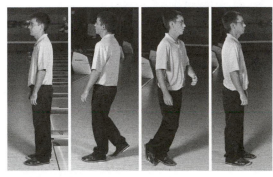

Figure 5-9, Distance from Foul Line

the starting distance from the foul line *(Figure 5-9)*. If they notice after a few shots that they are more than six inches from the foul line in the finish position, they will move their starting position closer. If they cross the foul line, they should make sure the first step is not too long (Refer to Chapter 6). If they find the first step to be OK, they should start slightly further away from the foul line.

Left/right position

To start with, it is recommended to line up on the Number 20 board, which is the big dot in the center. From there, changes can be made based on style, ball reaction and other factors. A right-handed bowler will line up with their left foot; a left-handed bowler will line up with their right foot *(Figure 5-10)*.

Physical Game Setup

In all areas of the physical game, coaches will look at the position in these four areas: waist down, waist up, ball position (in relation to the body) and hand position.

Stance

A good, balanced setup and stance is important to delivering a consistent shot. Bowlers must have a good start to have a good finish. The stance is to be relaxed and balanced *(Figure 5-11)*.

Waist down: Position the non-ball side foot on the desired board. Then place the other foot beside it and slightly back.

As the ball-side foot is dropped back, the hip should follow and end up slightly back. This position will help aid the armswing.

In order to execute a series of athletic movements, a bowler needs to flex their knees slightly as they line up in the stance *(Figure 5-11)*.

Waist up: To better prepare for moving forward and staying balanced, leaning forward

Figure 5-11, Knee Flex and Spine Position

Figure 5-12, Shoulder Drop Position

about 15 degrees will put the bowler's shoulders approximately over their knees. The bowler should maintain this upper-body position throughout the approach and delivery *(Figure 5-11)*.

Because the ball is heavy, it is only natural the shoulder on the ball side will be slightly lower than the other when relaxed *(Figure 5-12)*. If the spine becomes tilted too much because of the weight of the ball, the bowler should consider using a lighter ball.

Shoulders will be turned slightly because hips and feet have been turned open as well. By having the ball-side shoulder slightly back, it will create what is known as an "open" position. This position helps promote a good swing.

Ball Position: Bowlers should start with the ball approximately waist high and between the chin and shoulder. The opposite hand should be under the ball to help support the weight of the ball

Bowlers can adjust the height of the ball in the stance depending on foot tempo *(Figure 5-13)*. There are three

primary ball heights – waist high (as our baseline), and higher or lower positions.

Between the high and low positions, there are many different heights. It is important to know what position the ball is in by looking at the angle of the arm in relationship to the body. When necessary, bowlers can make slight modifications.

A quick foot tempo in the approach requires the bowler to lower the ball in the stance to maintain good timing. This will shorten the swing to help match tempo.

A slower foot tempo in the approach requires the bowler to raise the ball in the stance; this lengthens the swing to help match tempo.

Hand position: There are three basic wrist positions that a bowler can start with: relaxed, firm and strong *(Figure 5-14)*. In the stance, bowlers will choose one of the three to attain a particular type of release. The firm wrist is a good starting position for beginner bowlers.

To set the hand in a particular position, picture a clock face. If the bowler starts with the thumb pointing at 12 o'clock with a relaxed wrist *(Figure 5-14)*, then it will make it easier to roll a straight ball at the release.

To generate a slight curve, in the stance the bowler can place their hand into what is known as the "handshake" position with a firm wrist position. A right-handed bowler will place the thumb in the 10 o'clock position and a left-handed bowler will place the thumb in the 2 o'clock position. Another way to view this hand position is to imagine a bowler holding a bottle of water in front of them or a bowling bag by their side.

Figure 5-13, Ball Positions (l-r) low, medium, and high

Figure 5-14, Relaxed, firm and strong positions

THE BASIC APPROACH

The Four-Step Approach

Consistency and accuracy are the most important elements for success in bowling at any skill level. The four-step approach is recommended for the beginning bowler because it provides a solid foundation from which additional skills are added.

Having a good stance is the foundation for the approach. (Refer to Chapter 5).

The four-step approach consists of synchronizing the steps to the foul line with a relaxed ball swing. Timing is the term used to describe the relationship between where the ball is in relation to the body during the various steps.

While all the steps are presented separately, the goal is to have a smooth, fluid motion. This will take time and practice. Some irregular motions are to be expected while learning the approach.

For beginner bowlers, in each step "neutral" timing is recommended as a starting point as to where the ball should be in relationship to the feet. However, as skills increase and individual styles become more prominent, this timing may change somewhat. (Refer to Chapter 8).

Step 1: The first step *(Figure 6-1)*, is the most important because it sets the timing, direction, and balance necessary for the remaining steps.

The ball and the ball-side foot move out in sync with one another. This step needs to be the shortest one. All the remaining steps need to feel like they are building

in length and momentum so keep the first step short.

The ball is pushed slightly forward during the first step, about waist high, and then should be allowed to fall into the swing. This movement needs to be a relaxed, fluid movement.

Step 2: During the second step, the non-ball side foot moves forward as the ball arcs down *(Figure 6-1)*. The opposite hand that was helping support the weight of the ball moves away. At the end of the second step, the ball should be beside the body at, or slightly behind, the ball-side leg.

Step 3: The third step is taken with the ball-side foot *(Figure 6-1)*. The ball continues to swing back and at the end of the third step, the ball should be at its highest point in the backswing.

Let the ball swing back comfortably without forcing or pulling the ball higher. Pulling the ball back excessively can be the source of many problems including pulling

Figure 6-2, Follow Through

Figure 6-1, The Four Step Approach

the ball down into the forward swing causing the shoulders to over-rotate.

Step 4: During the fourth step, the non-ball side foot enters the slide as the ball swings forward *(Figure 6-1)*. The ball-side leg will begin to move over and behind the slide leg, making a clear path for the ball. The ball should be released at the lowest point of the swing, which would be at the ankle.

Follow Through

After completing the release, the arm should continue toward the target and then upward to where the hand ends up at least head high. This is just a continuation of the relaxed swing and not meant to be a muscled effort *(Figure 6-2)*. The ball-side leg will continue behind the slide leg with the toes preferably on the ground. Hold this balanced position until the ball hits the pins.

The Five-Step Approach

Sometimes it is easier to begin the approach with the non-ball side foot. In this case, a five-step approach can be used.

In this approach, the first step is with the non-ball side foot. This step is very small and the ball does not move. The second step becomes identical to the first step of the four-step approach with the ball-side foot and ball push-away in sync with one another. The rest of the approach mirrors the four-step approach *(Figure 6-3)*.

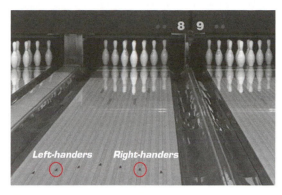

Figure 6-4, Second Arrow Targeting

Lane Targets

As the bowler takes their approach, it is advantageous to roll the ball to a target on the lane surface. Since the arrows are only about 15 feet from the foul line, they are easier to aim at; a common mistake made by most beginners is to focus on the pins (Refer to Chapter 2).

The second arrow from the channel is recommended as an initial target for strikes *(Figure 6-4)*, as it will provide a good angle into the pocket to achieve desired pin action. As skills improve and the ball begins to hook more, other targets may be more beneficial.

Bowlers may have to adjust their feet left or right from the Number 20 board to roll the ball over the second arrow and hit the pocket. When they do, this will become their new starting board. (Refer to Chapter 5).

While most bowlers prefer the arrows as targets, the lane locator dots also can be used successfully. A word of caution: most of these dots do not line up with the dots on the approach or the arrows. (Refer to Chapter 2).

Figure 6-3, The Five Step Approach

THE RELEASE

In bowling, the word "release" refers to the way the ball comes off the hand and onto the lane. As bowling skills improve, bowlers may want to learn multiple releases to change the way their ball rolls down the lane.

It is important to first put the fingers in the ball during the setup because if the thumb is put in first, or if the whole hand is put in at the same time, it can cause the thumb to shift slightly. This can cause the ball to come off the thumb inconsistently.

Wrist Positions

The three primary wrist positions that may be used to enhance the release are relaxed, firm and strong.

Many beginning bowlers have not developed the wrist strength to select and maintain these positions during the approach. With each of these wrist positions, the hand and wrist positions will be set in the stance and held in that position throughout the approach swing and until the point of release (Refer to Chapter 5). This method allows for a more consistent and controllable ball reaction.

Relaxed wrist position: The relaxed wrist position will decrease the ability of the ball to hook. In this position, the wrist is collapsed or bent away from the forearm *(Figure 7-1)*.

Firm wrist position: The firm wrist position is recommended for most beginning bowlers. In this position, the wrist is flat and in line with the back of the hand *(Figure 7-1)*

Strong wrist position: The strong wrist position is used to increase overall hook. The wrist is held in a position that is up and toward the forearm *(Figure 7-1)*.

Ball Rotation

Whether discussing the stance or release, visualize a clock hanging on a wall (Refer to Chapter 5). Although it is where the position of the fingers are at the release point that impart more or less RPM's (Revolutions Per Minute), it's the position of the thumb at the release that is the easiest way to explain the rotation of degrees given to a ball.

Figure 7-2 Straight Ball Release

Straight Ball

Bowlers should begin in the stance by pointing the thumb at 12 o'clock and the fingers at 6 o'clock with the thumb straight up. As the ball swings during the

Figure 7-1 Relaxed (left), Firm (middle) and the Strong (right) Wrist Position

Left Handed	Right Handed

Figure 7-3 Basic Hook Release

approach, it is important to keep the thumb pointing toward the pins. Picture the thumb pointing straight down the lane *(Figure 7-2)*. As the ball is being released, the thumb comes out first and the fingers roll the ball with the palm ending up pointing toward the ceiling. This will make the ball roll end over end or having little to no side rotation.

Basic Hook Release

In the stance, a right-handed bowler will place the thumb at 10 o'clock and the fingers at approximately 4 and 5 o'clock *(Figure 7-3)*. For a left-handed bowler, the thumb should be placed at 2 o'clock and the fingers at approximately 7 and 8 o'clock.

At the release, the thumb will come out of the ball first. Because the fingers are positioned slightly to the side of the ball and are in the ball for a split-second longer, they impart a slight side rotation on the ball which can be anywhere from 10 to 45 degrees; this is what makes the ball hook.

As with the straight ball, it is important to keep the thumb in the same position throughout the swing and release.

Basic Hook Release with Finger and Wrist Rotation

Once bowlers have developed control and accuracy with the basic hook release, they may be interested in developing a release that can produce a stronger ball reaction. In the stance, the wrist starts in the strong position. A right-handed bowler will start with their thumb at about 1 o'clock and the fingers at 7 or 8 o'clock and a left-handed bowler will position their thumb at about 11 o'clock and the fingers at 5 or 6 o'clock (Refer to Chapter 5).

Just as with the basic hook release, maintain hand position during the swing. At the point of release, the thumb exits and the wrist rotates causing the fingers to impart more side rotation to the ball; this can be anywhere from 45 to 90 degrees of rotation. A higher degree of rotation generates more hook potential.

Reverse Hook

A bowling ball with reverse hook (also called a back-up ball) will hook to the right for a right-handed bowler and to the left for a left-handed bowler.

At the release bowlers open their hand position so that the palm is facing up or forward. For a right-handed bowler, the thumb position is between 1 and 2 o'clock with the fingers at 6 or 7 o'clock. For a left-handed bowler, the thumb is between 10 and 11 o'clock with the fingers at 4 or 5 o'clock.

The thumb comes out of the ball first, and because the fingers are positioned slightly to the opposite side of the ball at release, it causes the ball to rotate in the opposite direction of a hook ball.

For the reverse hook to be used effectively, bowlers need to line up and play the lane like someone who rolls the ball with the opposite hand. For example, a right-handed bowler using a reverse hook will line up like a left-handed bowler.

The "No Thumb" Release

Not using the thumb in the ball has grown in popularity in recent years. This release is used with only the fingertips in the ball, palm flat on the ball, thumb on the outside of the ball, and the wrist in a strong position *(Figure 7-4)*. This requires a great deal of wrist

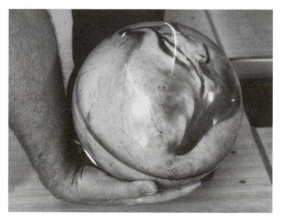

Figure 7-4 "No Thumb" Release

and forearm strength. It is also used for two-handed bowling, where the opposite hand stays on the ball just prior to the release (Refer to Chapter 14).

This release has the advantage of creating a great deal of hook. However, is it very difficult to control and repeat. It requires the development of good timing, a good armswing, and a balanced finish position.

Loft

Loft is the distance that the ball travels from the release point until it makes contact with the lane surface. Setting the ball down very close to the foul line is considered very little loft while a ball that lands out near the lane locator dots is considered excessive loft.

For most bowlers, it is ideal for the ball to first touch the lane approximately 10 to 20 inches beyond the foul line. Loft can be used to control hook, making the ball hook a little earlier or a little later down the lane.

Note: *Excessive loft is NOT recommended as the impact of the ball on the lanes can damage the lane surface.*

Common Release Problems

Many bowlers will start with either the firm or strong position only to have the wrist end up in the relaxed position during the approach and release. This usually occurs during the push-away, when a bowler extends the ball too far from the body and the forward momentum and weight of the ball makes the wrist collapse.

The most common release problems are the result of a poor-fitting ball. If the thumb hole is too tight, the thumb will not release cleanly. If the thumb hole is too loose, the ball can release too early and can cause the bowler to grip the ball more with their thumb. This can create an inconsistent release.

If a bowler develops blisters on their thumb or rubbing occurs, the hole is either too tight or too big.

Likewise, the span is just as important for a clean release. Stretching the hand to reach the holes puts undue strain on the hand and fingers making it difficult to achieve a good release.

Another problem occurs when bowlers try to "grab" or "lift" the ball to make it hook, this also makes it difficult to release the ball consistently.

DEVELOPING CONSISTENCY

Developing a consistent physical game should be the number one priority for a bowler. The ability to repeat a shot is important because it provides a base from where changes can be made. Whenever a change is made, it will take time to regain consistency so make changes one at a time and regain consistency before moving on to the next item.

Armswing

The most common area where beginning bowlers have consistency problems is the armswing. There are several potential causes for armswing problems including turned shoulders, poor timing, improper ball fit and wrong ball weight. Many of these issues can be identified and corrected in the stance and during the first step.

The initial ball movement should start about waist high and in line with the target path on the lane. If

Figure 8-1 Start In — Ball Out — Swing In

Figure 8-2 Start Out — Ball In — Swing Out

the ball is pushed up high, it can create too much momentum going into the backswing, causing the shoulder position and armswing direction to change. If the ball is pushed down low, it can cause the upper-body to bend over, making it harder to stay balanced for the duration of the approach and follow-through.

If the ball is pushed inward toward the body, the ball must avoid the leg going into the backswing and will likely swing out and away from the body and then back in across the body during the release *(Figure 8-1)*.

If the ball is pushed out away from the body, it will tend to swing in behind the back and then back out and away from the body during the release *(Figure 8-2)*. At times when the ball goes behind the back, the bowler may muscle or pull the ball around the torso and end up with the swing going across the body.

One way to correct an inconsistent swing *(Figure 8-3)* is to visualize a slot that the swing must stay in during the approach and release; this will keep the swing closer to the body *(Figure 8-4)*.

The swing should stay nice and relaxed. Once a good push-away can be executed, let gravity take over. A common tendency is to "muscle" the ball. This means that bowlers tend to either pull the ball up into the backswing or pull it down into the forward swing. The speed and momentum generated by the gravity of the ball, combined with the forward momentum of the body created by using the legs, is more than enough to generate good ball speed without involving too much muscle. The key is to have good swing direction, not force.

Shoulders / Torso

Following are three possible movements of the shoulders and torso. Although the shoulder will be dropped in the stance because of ball weight, it needs to be minimized (Refer to Chapter 5). If the torso is tilted too much at the waist, this will cause the shoulder to drop excessively. The second is the forward spine angle, or leaning too far forward, this can cause imbalance during the approach and finish position. The third, and most common, is the rotation of the torso which can create over-rotation of the shoulders; this can cause an inconsistent swing.

Dropped shoulder: In the stance, having the ball-side shoulder slightly dropped is fine because there is weight in the bowling hand. The problem is when the shoulder drops so much that it begins to cause a balance problem. At this point, the weight is to be evenly distributed on both feet. If most of the weight is on the ball-side foot, the torso might be tilted too much.

Sometimes the shoulder drop occurs during the approach. This usually happens as the ball is passing the knee going into the backswing. If this occurs, consider trying a lighter ball.

Forward spine angle: Excessive forward spine angle can start in the stance and is an easy fix. In the stance, the shoulders should be just about over the knees and the knees over the toes. As the ball goes into the backswing, too much forward spine angle can occur as the upper body will lean forward to act as a counter-balance for an excessively high backswing. It can also come from a lack of flexibility in the shoulders.

The opposite can occur as the ball goes into the downswing, where the upper body straightens or rears back just before the release. This can be caused from pulling the ball into the downswing.

Torso rotation: The most common movement of the shoulders is the rotation of the torso creating the shoulders to "open" or "close" during the approach. As the ball goes into the backswing, the torso can rotate causing the ball-side shoulder to move backward or "open". As the ball goes into the downswing, the ball-side shoulder will then have a tendency to "close" as the torso rotates causing the shoulder to move forward. This can cause bowlers to miss their intended target. To help

keep the shoulders and torso still during the approach, bowlers can concentrate on maintaining the same upper-body posture used in the stance throughout the approach.

Most bowlers begin their approach with their shoulders and torso square to the lane. This means their shoulders and torso are parallel with the foul line.

Depending on a bowler's style and technique, the bowling stance should start with the feet, torso and shoulders in a slightly open position. The focus here is on being square to the intended target path and not the lane (Refer to Chapter 5).

Drifting

During their approach, most bowlers drift or walk slightly sideways. Drift can be left or right, depending on the cause. For drift to be OK, it needs to be consistent from shot to shot. To ensure consistency, simply check starting position using the locator dots on the approach and then re-check in the finish position using the locator dots near the foul line. If it's not within three boards

Figure 8-3 Inconsistent Armswing

Figure 8-4, Consistent Armswing

from shot to shot, then consider it to be a possible item of concern.

Most drift occurs when the ball is moved outside of the slot that was discussed earlier; it also can be caused by the body's attempt to remain balanced.

Types of Timing

Timing is the measurement of where the ball is in relationship to the steps. Timing types are referred to as: Roller (previously known as early), Neutral (previously know as stroker), and Leverage (previously known as late).

Roller: Roller timing is when the ball is released before the non-ball side foot has stopped moving forward in the final step/slide or the ball is ahead of the feet in any given position. Bowlers with roller timing will have a tendency to lean forward going into the finish position.

Neutral: Neutral timing is when the ball is near the ankle of the non-ball side foot as it stops moving forward in the final step/slide or the ball is in the "4-step timing" position in any given step (Refer to Chapter 6).

Leverage: Leverage timing is when the ball is still in the downswing as the non-ball side foot stops moving in the final step/slide or the ball is behind the feet in any given position. Bowlers with leverage timing may end up rearing back with the torso going into the finish position.

Personal Timing

Avoid referring to timing as "good" or "bad" because timing should be somewhat different for various body types and bowling styles. For example, some styles should have leverage timing.

As beginning bowlers work to have sound basic skills, neutral timing is recommended (Refer to Chapter 6). The key to achieving this timing is to ensure that the ball and foot move in sync during the first step of the four-step approach. This means the ball goes forward with the movement of the first step; however, there needs to be separation between the ball and body.

Common Timing Problems

When a bowler pushes the ball out too far or pushes it down too fast, it can cause problems with upper-body posture and balance. This can also create issues in a bowler's personal timing if it does not sync with their footwork speed.

Timing is analyzed during each step. Bowlers can have specific types of timing on any given step. They may start with one type of timing then finish with different type of timing. This is what creates "personal" timing. What is right for one person might not be right for another.

The key to timing is to let the ball swing freely and in the slot. When changes in timing occur during the approach it is usually caused by the bowler muscling or pulling the ball during the swing.

Balance in the Finish Position

A bowler should be in balance at the finish position (*Figure 8-5*). When a bowler cannot hold their balance at the foul line, it's a good indication that something needs to be addressed during the approach.

When discussing balance in the finish position, the same four areas of waist down, waist up, ball position and hand position are used. These areas provide a framework for analyzing bowlers.

Waist Down

The non ball-side knee will be bent more here than in the stance, making the finish position lower. The ball-side leg (known as the trail leg) will move over behind the body, clearing a path for the armswing. It is recommended that the trail leg foot stay down on the approach; however, if the bowler can maintain balance, it is acceptable for the foot to finish off the approach in the air.

Waist Up

The spine angle of the upper body should be slightly forward with the shoulders and torso ending in the same position; head should remain still with eyes focused on the target while holding a balanced position until the ball hits the pins. This is important, as watching the ball go down the lane helps the bowler to know if they made a good shot or not. The bowling arm should swing from the shoulder and extend out and up, with the elbow ending at least head high.

Ball Position

At this point, the ball should be traveling down the lane. The bowler should remain in a balanced finish position and watch the ball as it rolls down the lane through the targets and take note of the ball's position in the front, midlane and backend as it rolls down the lane. This is the best way for the bowler to know if their physical game and armswing are consistent.

Hand Position

In terms of the clock-face position, the hand should finish in the same position that it ended with at the release.

Common Errors and Solutions

Topping the ball: If the thumb has rotated past 9 o'clock for a right-handed bowler or 3 o'clock for a left-handed bowler, the forearm and elbow may have over-rotated, causing the bowler to top the ball. "Topping" the ball can start at the release when the hand finishes on the top of the ball instead of below and on the side of the ball. If this happens, the bowler should focus on keeping their hand under the ball at the release point or keep their forearm facing forward all the way through the swing, release and follow through.

Not warming up before bowling: A bowler can have inconsistencies in the first few frames when they do not warm up. This is because the body tries loosening up during those frames. It can be the difference between a strike and a split (Refer to Chapter 5).

Not knowing starting and finish position: If starting position is off by one board, at the release the non ball-side foot/sliding foot will also be off. This causes inconsistency in the lay-down point of the ball each delivery, which may result as a three-board difference down the lane. If the starting and finishing position is unknown, it is difficult to make proper adjustments.

Controlling the swing: When a bowler is trying to be exact about hitting the target or trying to control the armswing, it tightens the muscles which can result in the bowler missing the intended target. Remember, the key is to keep the swing relaxed.

Not following through: When a bowler does not follow through, the ball might not have good direction or speed. A correct follow-through (Figure 8-5) will help assure that the ball reaches its intended target. Remember, it should be nothing more than a continuation of a loose armswing. Think about throwing a football — if the quarterback's hand stopped at the moment the football was released, then speed, distance and accuracy would be sacrificed.

Altering hand/wrist release position: For beginning bowlers, it is important to maintain the same hand and wrist position from the stance until the release. Varying the hand and/or wrist position during the approach can cause inconsistency in the ball's direction and reaction on the lane.

Figure 8-5 Back View of Finish Positions

Right foot slides toward the foul line

Left leg clears to the right

Left-Hand Bowler

Right leg clears to the left

Left foot slides toward the foul line

Right-Hand Bowler

Lane conditioner, also known as lane oil, is applied to the lane surface in various amounts and patterns which change with use and time. Understanding lane conditions, and why and what make lane conditions and oil patterns different, is essential to understanding the sport of bowling.

Lane conditioner is more commonly known as "oil" and in bowling these terms are used interchangeably.

In most bowling centers today, there are specialized machines that will strip (clean) and oil the lanes at the same time. Lane machines have computers that are programmed in precise increments regarding where and how much oil to apply to the lane. Often, these machines cost as much as a new car.

Usually, a bowling center will strip each lane at least once a day. This process includes removing any conditioner that is on the lane along with dust and dirt that has accumulated.

After each lane is cleaned, fresh conditioner is applied. The most common distances start from a few inches past the foul line and run anywhere from 32 to 44 feet down the lane. The combination of the distance, volume (amount applied) and the ratio across the lane from the middle to outside boards is known as an oil pattern. Random inspections of the oil applied to lanes in bowling centers are performed to ensure they meet USBC guidelines for oil application. Most bowling centers use a "house" pattern in which more conditioner is applied to the middle of the lane than the outside edges *(Figure 9-1)*, primarily because this area of the lane is used more often.

Purposes of Lane Conditions

There are two reasons lane conditioner is used: to protect the lane's surface from damage and to regulate the level of difficulty.

The playing field in the sport of bowling remains fairly constant. It's a game played indoors. The lane is the same size from building to building, city to city, state to state and even internationally. However, the lane conditioner is clear, which makes the oil pattern invisible. It is important to understand why and how conditioner is applied to the lanes and, as skills increase, there will be a need to understand what happens to the oil pattern and how it affects the reaction of the ball on the lane.

The playing field is continually changing. Factors such as humidity, heat and air conditioning affect the oil pattern as well as bowling balls picking up and moving conditioner around on the lane.

Protects the Surface

At times, bowling balls accumulate oily residue. This is the lane conditioner that was applied to the lane. The conditioner helps protect the lane surface by reducing the friction from the bowling balls. It allows the ball to skid on the lane surface before hooking into the pins.

Think of lane conditioner in these terms: the more conditioner there is on the lane, the less friction there is between the ball and the lane surface. With less conditioner comes more friction. With more friction, there is a greater potential for the ball to hook.

From this perspective, the conditioner will protect the lanes because it reduces the friction and potential damage to the lane surface.

Regulates the Level of Difficulty

Where and how much conditioner is applied to the lane affects the level of difficulty in bowling.

The volume (amount) of conditioner applied on the lane can provide some answers to help understand ball reaction. Conditioner can be applied to make it easier or difficult to hook the ball into the pocket.

There are other factors which can affect the reaction of the ball such as the brand and deterioration of the lane surface, the topography of the lane, the center's lane maintenance program and the climate control in the bowling center.

Another way to view the difficulty of the oil pattern is to imagine a golf course with the sand traps and water hazards being invisible. On a bowling lane, it is difficult to tell where the oily and dry areas are until a bowler rolls a ball down the lane. By watching the reaction of a bowling ball, it will help the bowler figure out where the oily and dry areas are on the lane.

The basic types of lane conditions include: Dry, medium and oily. While lane conditions are discussed in general terms, there are many variations in between each of them.

Each condition will require bowlers to adjust from their normal starting position to compensate for differing amounts of friction (Refer to Chapter 10).

Dry lanes: A lower volume or a dry lane has less lane conditioner on the lane surface. A dry lane increases the friction between the ball surface and the lane, resulting in a ball that hooks earlier or more than expected.

Medium lanes: A medium volume of conditioner placed on the lane is favorable for most styles, requiring small adjustments when necessary.

Oily lanes: A higher volume of conditioner or an oily lane has more conditioner on the lane surface. Sometimes referred to as being "flooded", this presence of oil reduces the amount of friction between the ball surface and lane, resulting in a ball that hooks later or less than expected.

Lane Oil Patterns

Within the types of lane conditions are specific patterns. Today's patterns are designed off of oil length, volume and width ratios. The length is, of course, the distance of the pattern from just past the foul line to the designated distance down the lane. The volume is the quantity of oil used for a pattern. Ratios are how much of that oil is placed across the width of the lane. A "house" or recreation pattern can have a width ratio of 10 to 1 with the "10" representing the center of the lane where the higher concentration of oil is placed, and the "1" representing the outside portion of the lane.

House Pattern: A standard "house" pattern is used in an effort to satisfy a wide range of customers – not too challenging or too easy. The "house" condition is usually in the medium volume range. This lane condition is commonly set up for league bowling and weekend recreational bowlers. However, depending on the bowling center's lane surface and the proprietor's discretion, it can range from dry to oily *(Figure 9-1)*.

Blocked is a term from the past. A "blocked" lane refers to lanes that have been set up for optimum scoring. This pattern will have significantly more oil in the center with less applied to the outside areas and, in effect, will maneuver the ball toward the pocket. These patterns can produce more strikes and higher scores.

Another term from the past is a "reverse block" pattern. Although this type of pattern is not seen much in today's game, bowlers still come across one now and then. When it comes to scoring, it is extremely difficult. With a reverse block, there is more oil on the outsides of the lane and less oil in the middle of the lane.

The "reverse" block can appear to emerge after a lot of games have been bowled and the oil from the middle of the lane has been depleted. A reverse block is not usually an intentional lane condition but one that is created by a combination of carry down and oil breakdown. It takes skill to conquer this condition.

Sport Pattern: Sport patterns were designed to promote and reward good shot-making which requires the bowler to have a sound physical game. The ratio for these patterns is no greater than 3 to 1 which makes the pattern flatter across the lane *(Figure 9-2)*. USBC created the challenging lane conditions for bowlers who wanted separation from the recreational point of view. As in any sport, the elite needed a way to distinguish themselves. Sport Bowling rolled out as a league option in the 2002-03 season.

Sport patterns are far more challenging than most house patterns. Statistics have shown bowlers will average less on sports patterns than on house patterns, so a special average chart was created that makes adjustments for the differences between the two (this chart can be found at BOWL.com).

On Sport patterns, the ball will not be redirected to the strike pocket as it can be with a house pattern. Because of this, it is up to the bowler to be more accurate with their shot-making.

Coming across a Sport pattern may be difficult unless the proprietor is asked to develop a Sport league. Bowling on these challenging patterns is worth the effort, as it requires physical and emotional control.

Breakdown

Breakdown is the deterioration of the lane conditioner on the surface of the bowling lane. Lane conditioner begins to evaporate as soon as it is applied to the lane and breakdown happens over the course of use or time, whether it's a couple of games or several hours.

While bowling, a bowler may see their bowling ball react differently from shot to shot. One explanation for this might be, after a bowler has bowled a few games or a team of bowlers has rolled a few frames, the conditioner was reduced or moved around, making the challenge not only an invisible one but one that's ever changing.

The most prevalent reason for breakdown is use. The more that a lane is bowled on, the more the oil dissipates. Bowling balls can push or pick up oil and carry it to the backend of the lane, the pin deck, and the underground ball return track. Also, if the bowling ball is made from reactive resin, the small amounts left can get absorbed into the ball.

When bowling in league, bowlers will experience lane patterns breaking down. Here is a scenario and solution: A basic shot has been rolled down the second arrow. The bowler has not had many problems getting the ball to the pocket. Then in the middle of the first game, a shot is rolled and the ball reacts differently (i.e. hooks more or less). On the next shot, the bowler will make an adjustment by moving their feet a few boards in the direction of the miss and the ball is back in the pocket once again. This is a typical solution for breakdown on a house pattern. The best thing to do when patterns break down is make adjustments. (Refer to Chapter 10). By watching other bowlers that are similar in style, it is possible to see where they're rolling the ball and if what they're doing is working or not. Experience along with knowledge will help adjustment decisions be smarter and quicker over time.

Carry Down

Carry down refers to oil that has "carried" further down the lane once bowling has taken place.

Conditioner is applied at a specific distance down the lane and this distance will differ from bowling center to bowling center. Carry down occurs as a ball rolls through the front part of the lane, where the application of the oil is usually the highest, and the ball pushes and picks up that oil carrying it down the lane. It can leave small traces of it on the drier surface at the backend. This is similar to a tire going through a puddle, where water is picked up by the tire and deposited later. Just as the track of a tire can be seen on pavement, if one looks close enough the track of a ball can also be seen on the lane.

Carry down has two opposite effects. First, since oil is removed and pushed from the front of the lane where the ball is being rolled, as time goes on that area will have less conditioner and increased friction. This increased friction creates earlier hook. Second, because the oil was carried and pushed farther towards the middle and back of the lane, this can cause a slight build up of the conditioner in this area, decreasing friction which causes the ball to skid farther down the lane.

Depending on the type and deterioration of the lane surface, the oil carry down might be more obvious and take place faster. On some lanes, the carry-down effects are not even noticeable.

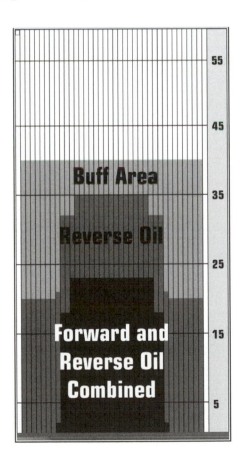

Figure 9-1 House Pattern

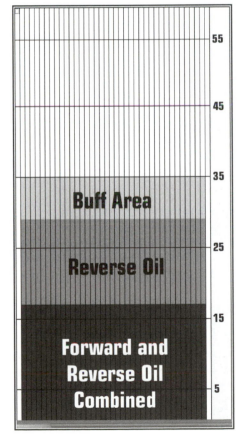

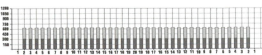

Figure 9-2 Sport Pattern

MAKING ADJUSTMENTS

Bowlers learn to make sound adjustments with their feet, target, hand release and bowling balls. Adjusting will maximize scoring potential on varying lane patterns and changing conditions.

The Starting Position

The most important part of making an adjustment is to understand the starting position and how to line up (Refer to Chapter 5).

Using a slight hook (Refer to Chapters 6 and 7) provides a good starting point for hitting the pocket on a house pattern.

However, this starting position and target is not guaranteed to be the right one for everyone. Why is the second-arrow method used if it doesn't always work? The second arrow is used as a base upon which adjustments can be made.

When making adjustments, it is important to know the bowler's starting position; this way it gives the bowler a starting place from which to make adjustments. For example, if it's suggested that a bowler move two boards one direction or another and didn't know exactly where they started the previous shot, the adjustment would not be effective.

Adjustments will be necessary at some point. Knowing this and being prepared to make these adjustments will give an edge over bowlers who are not prepared to make changes. Adjustments are not just made at the start of a new game; often, changes are required several times during a game, and in competition the victory usually goes to the bowler who is able to quickly recognize and make those changes.

Adjustments with Feet

Moving the feet on the approach remains the most common adjustment in bowling. For beginners, moving the feet in the direction of the miss and using a different target arrow are great ways to make adjustments.

Moving in the direction of the miss: The bowler's "Golden Rule" is to move the feet the direction that the ball missed at the pins, keeping the target the same on the lane *(Figure 10-1)*.

The concept of this adjustment is based on the use of a pivot, with the pivot being the target on the lane. If the ball misses to the left of the intended pin(s) (Path "A" in illustration), the feet move left on the approach (Path "B" in illustration). If the ball misses to the right of the intended pin(s) the feet should move right on the approach.

Changing the starting position (right or left) on the approach and delivering the ball at the same target on the lane is known as an angular change. By delivering a ball from an adjusted starting position, the result is the ball intersecting the target at a different angle. This new angle represents an adjustment to the previous path the ball made over the target.

After moving the feet right or left on the approach, a bowler should remember to align their body to the new target line to complete the angular change. If the target was missed, the bowler needs to understand the angular path was not changed and they created a different ball path. In this case, the bowler waits until they roll a good shot over the target before making any other adjustments.

The adjustment size depends on how much the original shot missed the pocket or intended pin. If the ball missed the pocket by one to two boards, a subtle one or two board adjustment with the feet should be sufficient. If the ball missed the intended pin by three or more boards, a larger adjustment must be made with the feet.

For example, the first shot rolls over the second arrow perfectly and the ball hooks too early, crossing over to hit dead center on the headpin, therefore missing the pocket by approximately three boards. This is known as a "high" hit *(Figure 10-2)*. For a right-handed bowler, this would be missing to the left of the 1-3 pocket; for a left-hander, this would mean missing to the right of the 1-2 pocket.

The adjustment would be to move the feet three boards on the approach. A right-handed bowler will move to the left and a left-handed bowler would move to the right. On the next attempt, the shot rolls over the second arrow again and hits the strike pocket, but the

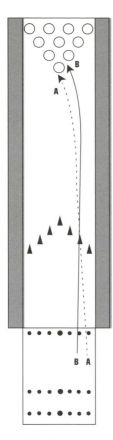

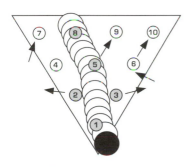

Figure 10-1, Move in Direction of Miss

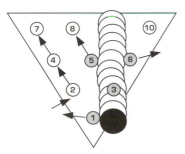

ball does not hit the head pin as much as desired. This is known as a "light" hit *(Figure 10-3)*. This would mean that a right-handed bowler missed slightly right and a left-hander, slightly left.

Prior to rolling the third shot, they move their feet the other direction one board. A right-handed bowler will move back to the right and a left-handed bowler moves back to the left, which makes their original move now two boards. On this shot, the bowler strikes. Now they are once again lined up so the ball enters the pocket. Angular adjustments are made after a bowler has found an area on the lane that will work for them and they will continually fine-tune that area.

Using a different target arrow: To take full advantage of the present lane condition, bowlers might have to move from the second-arrow target line. This might involve moving both the feet and target on the lane.

While the move described above is an angular move, when moving to a different part of the lane, initially it is made as a parallel move. In a parallel move, the feet and target move the same amount and direction *(Figure 10-4)*. Using the example above, imagine the bowler started their stance standing on the middle dot (the number 20 board) and their target was the second arrow (the number 10 board). If the bowler moves to stand on the next dot (the number 25 board) and targets at the third arrow (the number 15 board), this is a five-board parallel move.

Parallel adjustments are typically made when bowlers are searching the lane for an area to play that will allow them to be comfortable and hit the pocket.

Altering the Release

Another way to make adjustments for lane conditions is by altering the release. By using the different wrist positions (Refer to Chapters 5 and 7), bowlers can change the way a ball rolls.

If a bowler encounters dry lanes and the ball is hooking too much, they can make an adjustment to the wrist position. Using the relaxed wrist position will generate fewer revolutions to the ball and reduce the overall hook of the ball.

The opposite is true if a bowler comes across an oily lane condition. If the ball is going too straight, the bowler can use the strong wrist position to increase RPMs and generate more side rotation. This will help increase the hook potential.

Adjusting Speed

Making an adjustment with ball speed is another variable that can be used to control hook. A bit more or less speed will increase or reduce the amount of time a ball has to make a change of direction. This adjustment can be very effective; nevertheless, it is difficult to master without affecting the armswing.

To increase ball speed slightly, bowlers hold the ball lower in the stance (Refer to Chapter 5) and increase the speed of their legs and feet. This shorter swing syncs with the faster speed of the legs and foot work and, in turn, generates more ball speed. To decrease the speed, bowlers hold the ball higher in the stance (Refer to Chapter 5) and decrease the speed of the legs and feet. This longer swing-plane syncs with the slower speed

Figure 10-2, High Hit (Right Handed)

Figure 10-3, Light Hit (Right handed)

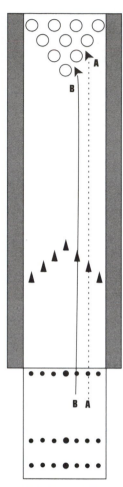

Figure 10-4, Parallel Move

of the legs and footwork, thus decreasing ball speed. This change of pace with the feet and ball height helps to maintain a relaxed swing.

Common errors made by bowlers are when they try to control "faster" or "slower" by using muscles and/or body position. Making the ball height adjustment in the stance and increasing or decreasing the leg and footwork speed makes the adjustment easier to accomplish. If bowlers find this difficult, it is recommended to make adjustments by adjusting the feet left or right; it is easier to do and can produce the desired results.

Altering the Ball Surface

Another option for adjusting to lane conditions is by altering the surface of the bowling ball. However, changing the ball's surface is prohibited during competition. Changing the ball's surface can be accomplished by sanding or polishing it (Refer to Chapter 3).

Sanding a ball will make the surface rougher, creating more traction and causing the ball to hook earlier. Conversely, polishing a ball will make the surface smoother, reducing traction and causing the ball to skid longer and hook later. Using different sanding grits and polishing compounds is the most effective way for bowlers to change the surface and ball reaction.

It is recommended that bowlers visit their local International Bowling Pro Shop and Instructors Association (IBPSIA) certified pro shop professional to perform the sanding and polishing, as they have the proper equipment and expertise needed to fine-tune the reaction of bowling balls.

Reasons to Make Adjustments

Lane conditions: Differing amounts of conditioner applied to various areas of the lane, as well changing lane conditions during a match, requires bowlers to make adjustments (Refer to Chapter 9).

The bowler: Every individual has a unique bowling style. Most likely, each style will translate into differences in their bowling ball reaction on the lane. It is up to each individual to know their style and adjust accordingly.

Equipment: The bowling ball's surface strongly affects ball reaction. Using bowling balls with different surfaces or changing the surface is an adjustment bowlers can use to get the desired ball reaction.

The easiest way to raise a bowling score is through the conversion of spares.

The basic spare-shooting method is known as the "3–6–9" spare conversion system. There are other systems for making spares but the 3-6-9 method is simple and easy to use. All spare conversion systems follow three steps:

1. Identify the key pin.
2. Align the feet on the approach to a new starting position.
3. Square the body to the target on the lane.

Step 1: Identify the Key Pin

There are hundreds of possible spare conversion combinations that a bowler might face. In each case, a spare conversion opportunity will have a specific pin that the ball must initially hit to increase the chances of converting the spare. This pin is known as the "key pin." The key pin will be the pin closest to the bowler (*Figure 11-1*).

To help convert spares, bowlers should know the pin numbering system (Refer to Chapter 2) or the diagrams in this chapter.

Instead of seeing a cluster of pins, bowlers should view each spare as a single-pin spare conversion. This creates the best opportunity to make the spare.

To maximize spare conversions, bowlers need to understand how the ball impacts the pins. This way they will be able to adjust where they want the ball to hit the key pin – left, right or middle.

Located directly behind the 1, 2 and 3 pins are the 5, 8 and 9 pins; these are known as "sleeper" pins since they can't be seen easily and are not usually key pins. If the 5, 8, or 9 becomes the key pin, the adjustments to convert the spare are based off the pin number directly in front of it.

Understanding where the key pin fits into the overall scheme is important for converting the spare.

Spare Zones: The pins or pin deck are divided into seven specific spare zones (*Figure 11-1*). Note that there are three zones to the right and to the left of the head pin.

By using a key pin, it will increase the possibility of the ball hitting the pins. A bowling ball can miss the intended target left or right and still hit the key pin. This is because of the range or coverage that a ball has to hit the pin (*Figure 11-2*).

However, not every spare combination has a key pin standing to help the bowler align their shot for the spare conversion; this is the "baby split" exception. With a baby split, the ball must fit between two pins to convert the spare. Examples of this type of spare conversions are the 3–10, 2–7, 4-5 and 5-6 spare combinations. In this case, the bowler needs to align the shot with the pin that would have been between or in front of the gap between the pins. The 4-pin is the key pin to convert the 2-7 spare. Likewise, the 6-pin is the key pin to picking up the 3-10.

Splits: When faced with splits that are wider than the baby split, there is a decision to be made. If the pins are in the same row, the bowler should choose the pin they are most comfortable with as it is difficult to hit one pin and slide it straight across the pin deck into the other pin. If the pins are not in the same row, the bowler should aim for the pin that is the closest to them and try to hit the far edge of the pin. Because the pins are in different rows, it creates an angle which will give them an opportunity to slide the pin across the deck into the other pin standing.

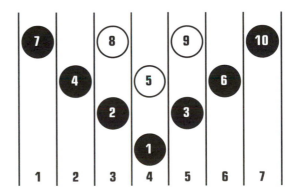

Figure 11-1, Key Pin Positions and Seven Spare Zone

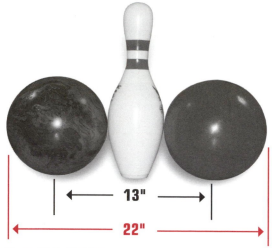

Figure 11-2, Pin Coverage

13"

22"

Step 2: Aligning the Feet on the Approach to a New Starting Position

Once the bowler has lined up for strikes and knows their starting position, the next step is for the bowler to figure out how much, and in what direction, they need to move from that position in order to hit the key pin and convert the spare. Converting spares will become a matter of changing the strike line angle on the lane. The 3–6–9 spare conversion system is based on the concept of changing the angle of the ball path.

Basic moves: To increase the margin for error and still convert the spare, spares are made by shooting "cross lane." That is, instead of rolling the ball parallel with the boards in line with the key pin, it will be rolled from an angle. For key pin shots to the right of the head pin, the starting position moves left. For the key pins to the left of the head pin, the starting position moves right.

The spare adjustment chart *(Figure 11-3)* reveals that for each zone away from the head pin, the bowler moves three boards per zone either right or left; so the bowler will move either three, six or nine boards with their feet from their starting position. The system's name is derived from these incremental moves. In the 3-6-9 system, bowlers continue to use the same target on the lane as their strike ball.

Step 3: Square the Body to the Target on the Lane

After a bowler has made the adjustment to the right or left on the approach, they will angle their body toward

the target to complete the angle change necessary to convert the spare *(Figure 11-4)*. This angle includes the feet, hips and shoulders all being turned slightly so that the bowler is facing the target. As noted earlier, in this system the target on the lane does not move. The bowler continues to aim at the target used to get strikes. As the bowler begins their approach, they will walk toward the target. This may mean walking diagonally in relation to the boards. This diagonal approach will keep them parallel to the intended ball path.

Key or single pin conversion	Adjustment on approach	Board number of new starting position (right-handed bowler)	Board number of new starting position (left-handed bowler)
1 (5)	none	20	20
2 (8)	three boards right	17	23
4	six boards right	14	26
7	nine boards right	11	29
3 (9)	three boards left	23	17
6	six boards left	26	14
10	nine boards left	29	11

Figure 11-3, Spare Adjustment Chart

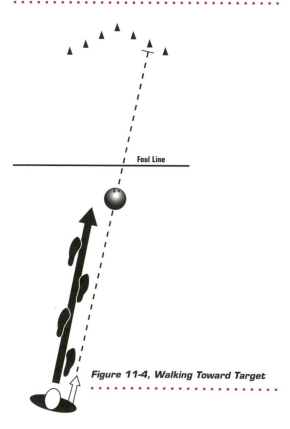

Foul Line

Figure 11-4, Walking Toward Target

THE MENTAL GAME

An often overlooked component of bowling is the mental game. This element is far more important than investing in more equipment.

It is important to understand that each shot is an independent event and any previous shots have nothing to do with the potential outcome of the ones to follow.

The human mind is so complex that once a bowler has rolled at least one strike, the brain sends the message that they have the ability to roll another one.

Staying Positive

There is no doubt that bowling, like any sport, can be frustrating. There are times when all bowlers have made what they think looks like a great strike shot only to leave a pin standing. Then they adjust their feet and line up to make the spare conversion and miss it by an inch. Meanwhile, another bowler rolls a shot that misses the target and seems to get a lucky break.

All bowlers will experience these events; it is how they deal with such events that make the difference. Bowlers need to be positive to ensure each shot is executed to its full potential.

Negative comments should be avoided as they can become self-fulfilling. When a bowler says "I can't get a strike or spare," they usually prove themselves right by missing the target or spare.

When bowlers focus on positive results by using self talk before they step onto the approach – saying "I can do this!" – they relax and make better shots and prove themselves right in a positive way.

Visualization and Positive Mental Imagery

Visualization and positive imagery are powerful mental tools. These concepts program the mind and set the tone for each delivery.

When bowlers visualize successfully accomplishing a specific task, such as a perfect shot or converting a spare, they are setting the stage to do exactly that. For example, a specific task would be a bowler visually seeing themselves in a perfect stance, finish position or a having a loose armswing. They place that picture in their mind before stepping on the approach, then step up to make it happen.

Imagery sometimes takes the form of a daydream. It can be a "playback" from previous events or something that has not been done before. When bowlers imagine rolling the ball over their target and into the pocket for a strike, it is known as the "line in the mind." This imagery technique is done by imagining a line drawn on the lane through the target into the pocket. Once the bowler delivers the ball, they watch it and see it roll down that line. Imagery is a very powerful tool simply because seeing the process reinforces the belief in it.

Focus on the Process, Not the Outcome

Bowlers tend to spend too much time worrying about their final score. In the history of bowling, there has never been a single pin added by focusing on the score bowled. However, future scores can improve by focusing on the process of the next shot.

When bowlers step on the approach, they should stay focused on the target or intended ball path on the lane. It has been proven that imagery will help bowlers focus on what they need to do to achieve success during the approach and delivery.

Think of process and outcome this way. A person is driving a car and they see a curve ahead. Do they simply think "curve ahead" or does the mind think about the process of turning the wheel the correct amount and direction? The outcome is getting around the curve. The process was turning the wheel.

When applied to bowling, bowlers cannot get a strike by simply saying, "I want a strike." Before they set up on the approach, they need to contemplate the process of their approach. Once they set up in the stance, their focus should be on where they want the ball to roll. If a bowler stands too long waiting to roll a shot, they can start to think too much and the body will tense up which can lead to a poorly-executed shot.

Controlling Emotions

Bowling is challenging and exciting when goals are reached and high scores are achieved. In any sport, getting upset will not help the outcome and getting too excited can create problems as well.

Loud outbursts and kicking or hitting equipment are a distraction for others getting ready to bowl. Of course, it's okay to celebrate when things go well; however, bowlers should be courteous so it doesn't affect others.

If a bowler rolls a bad shot, it's understandable they would be upset but they need to get it out of their mind to allow themselves to make a better shot in the next frame. If thoughts are focused on a previous bad shot, it makes it hard to concentrate on making the current shot. Being angry also causes the muscles to tense, making it difficult to relax and repeat shots.

Getting overly excited can cause distraction and keep bowlers from focusing on the task at hand. For bowlers to keep a good game going, they should focus on the process of executing a good shot instead of what the score is or will be.

Setting Goals

Another powerful psychological tool that a bowler can use to improve their game is goal setting. If bowlers are willing to work hard and practice, then by properly setting and documenting goals the bowlers can achieve any level they desire.

When setting goals, it is essential to strive for an improvement in performance, not the outcome of a game or event. For a goal to succeed, bowlers must have complete control over the accomplishment. For example, increasing an individual average by 10 pins is obtainable. Winning a league or tournament has factors such as teammates, performance and the strength of other competitors that cannot be controlled.

Often, goals are set too high because of outside influences. Parents, friends or teammates may expect a higher level of performance but each individual should be the only one setting goals for themselves. It's all right for others to offer advice, but the one receiving that advice should not be pressured into unrealistic goals.

Here is a good acronym for goals:
Growth-focused
Obtainable
Action-oriented
Listed and prioritized
Specific

Growth-focused: A goal isn't a goal if it doesn't motivate a person to improve. A goal is set as a means to measure progress in whatever endeavor is being pursued. Bowling is a perfect sport for setting goals. Bowlers can seek short-term goals, such as beating their average during league play, or perhaps a long-term goal of reaching a 200-plus average.

Obtainable: Goals must be realistic. If the goal seems beyond grasp, it can become a source of frustration instead of motivation. When it seems as though goals might be too easy, bowlers should set them higher to motivate further improvement.

Action-oriented: Setting goals is not deciding what to accomplish and then waiting for it to happen. The purpose of a goal is to motivate people into taking action to achieve the desired goal. Each goal must have an action plan. These types of questions will help:
• Where can instructional materials be obtained?
• Will additional or new equipment be needed?
• Where can bowlers find coaching?
• What can impede the bowler's progress?

Answering these questions allows bowlers to think through their plan and to know that they can accomplish the goal.

Listed and prioritized: All the goals should be listed and prioritized. By writing down goals, bowlers get a sense of commitment and a clear understanding of what is to be accomplished. By assigning priorities, they may find that working toward high-priority goals will help to achieve other goals. For example, a bowler having a priority goal of making two more spares a game can help them achieve an average goal.

Specific: Each goal must be specific and measurable. This is a step that must be carefully thought through. If a goal has no time frame or can't be measured, it is not likely to be taken seriously. For instance, setting a goal of increasing an average by 10 pins is measurable, but taking two years to do it (unless the bowler already has a 220-plus average) may not be that challenging.

To create good specific goals, ask these questions:
What is the specific goal or accomplishment?
When will it be accomplished? Set a date.
Where is the place this goal needs to be accomplished?
    (a center, league or tournament)
How is the goal to be achieved and what actions are
    necessary to accomplish the goal?

Practicing the techniques mentioned will help bowlers realize that improvements in their physical game, bowling score and overall mental attitude are obtainable.

ADAPTIVE SKILLS

Bowling is a sport easily adapted for people who have special needs and physical limitations. The ease of adaptability is one reason why bowling is a favorite activity among people with physical limitations. Bowling is one of the most popular sports in the Special Olympics.

There are many organizations that promote or have various tournaments and events for bowlers using adaptations. Special Olympics has an entire guide on adaptive skills and working with Special Olympic athletes. It is highly recommended that anyone wishing to assist these athletes read the organization's guide.

Regardless of the type of athlete, the information provided in this book is valuable to all bowlers. For example, warming up and stretching is important, perhaps even more important, for challenged bowlers. Sometimes there are unique formats and rules when using adaptive equipment. For instance, in some cases a bowler will be allowed to complete two or more frames while in position at the foul line before the next bowler takes their turn.

This chapter covers some of the adaptations needed for bowlers in a wheelchair or who have limited vision.

Wheelchair Bowling

Many of today's centers are being designed and constructed with a level surface between the concourse, bowler's area and approach to make it easier for those in wheelchairs to access the lanes. Older centers have ramps and lifts designed to provide access for the bowlers.

As bowlers enter the area in their wheelchair, they should take a moment to make sure the wheels are clean and dry to avoid endangering others. Bowlers who have upper-body strength and coordination can choose to roll one-handed while leaning over the side of the chair. Some bowlers will use a specific ramp – a portable device which can be placed near the foul line – to help play the game. Ramps have a small level area at the top on which a ball is placed, and then continues into a sharply angled slope that helps accelerate the ball as it is pushed from the top.

With a Ramp

When bowling with a ramp, the bowler positions the ramp on the approach then moves it left or right to create the desired launch angle *(Figure 13-1)*. Generally, it is placed so that the center (large) dot of the approach at the foul line is directly between the two rails. The end of the ramp should not touch or go beyond the foul line as this will be considered a foul. In official Special Olympics competition, if an assistant positions the ramp, the location must be indicated by the bowler either verbally or by sign.

When the ramp and bowler are in position, the ball is placed at the top of the ramp *(Figure 13-1)*. It is recommended that the holes face upward with the

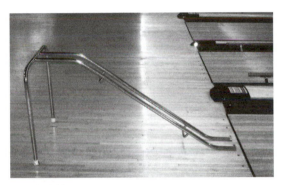

Figure 13-1, Bowling Ramp and Ball Position on Ramp

When using a ramp, it should be positioned so that the center (large) dot of the approach is directly between the two sloped rails.

Position the bowling ball on the ramp with the holes facing upward. The finger holes should be toward one hand and the thumb hole toward the other hand.

Figure 13-2, Wheelchair Bowling Without a Ramp

Wheelchair bowling without a ramp requires the bowler to lean to one side of the chair and execute a one-handed delivery.

finger holes toward one hand and the thumb hole toward the other hand. This is because the area in the middle of the grip is slightly heavier than other parts of the ball. Placing the heavy spot right or left will cause the ball to hook. Having the fingers and thumb to the sides will allow the ball to roll without hitting the holes. When the ball rolls over the holes it can cause the ball to "jump" and veer off the intended path.

There are three methods for making spares using a ramp.

The first method is to move the entire ramp left or right so that it is in line with the key pin. The second method is to slightly angle the ramp by moving the back of the ramp left or right and leaving the front of the ramp in the strike position. The third method is to turn the ball on the top of the ramp so that the imbalance of the ball will cause it to hook into the pins. A word of caution – bowlers should use slight adjustments as the imbalance of the ball can create a surprisingly big effect on the ball's reaction (Refer to Chapter 11).

If the next bowler does not need the ramp, the best place to store the ramp between uses is in front of the ball return.

Without a Ramp

Many wheelchair bowlers with sufficient upper-body strength prefer to bowl without a ramp because of the increased control of the ball. Basically, this involves the bowler leaning to one side of the chair and executing a one-handed delivery *(Figure 13-2)*.

To begin, a bowler picks up the ball from the ball return and places it in their lap; then they roll the chair into position at the foul line. Some bowlers have a special attachment on their chairs designed to hold the ball while they get into position at the foul line.

When lining up on the approach, the bowler moves the chair left or right so that the path of the ball swing will be in line with their target on the lane. This might mean having the chair at a slight angle toward the target line. Many bowlers move the front of the chair into

position last so that the front wheels are not blocking the ball path.

Before beginning the swing and release, bowlers should make sure the wheel locks are set tight as the momentum from the swinging ball can sometimes alter the chair's position. If necessary, have an assistant help to hold the chair in position. A seat belt may be helpful if the bowler is shifting in the chair during the delivery.

For the bowler to initiate the swing, they should place the ball in the hand used for the delivery and lean enough to the side for the ball to swing without hitting the chair. On some chairs, the side rail and arm rest can be removed to make it easier to swing the ball. If the bowler needs extra support or stability, they can hold onto the arm rest on the other side of the chair with their opposite hand.

The bowler should position their hand using one of three wrist positions (Refer to Chapters 5 and 7) to achieve the amount of hook desired. It might be helpful for the bowler to rest the ball on the approach, place the hand in the ball and set the wrist in position before lifting the ball to initiate the swing.

For the swing, it is recommended the bowler hold the ball straight down to their side. Once ready, the bowler gives a slight forward push toward the pins and allows the arm to swing back easily without pulling it. Then they allow the arm to swing forward and release the ball toward the target on the lane.

Figure 13-3, Bowling with a Rail

A rail is a common piece of adaptive equipment for visually impaired bowlers

Spare shooting may be accomplished by adjusting the position of the chair similar to the spare shooting system (Refer to Chapter 11).

Visually-Impaired Bowlers

Bowlers with limited or no sight rely on their sense of touch and the assistance of others to get positioned on the approach and make the delivery. Many bowlers develop the ability to approximate how many pins fell by listening to the impact of the ball as it hits the pins.

It is difficult to visualize angles, so most will line up so their swing and release will go straight for all their deliveries, including spares. These bowlers will need a spotter to let them know what pins, if any, are standing after the delivery of the first ball. Bowlers with limited sight will require some amount of assistance in lining up and spare shooting.

With a Rail

A common piece of adaptive equipment for visually-impaired bowlers is a rail *(Figure 13-3)*. This rail will run from the back of the approach to the foul line. The bowler will loosely hold or otherwise keep contact with the rail while bowling to ensure the approach is straight.

To use the rail, the bowler positions themselves at the foul line a set distance away from the rail. A spotter can help them to line up with the target on the lane. They can then either hook their elbow over the bar as a guide or rely on feel to remember the amount of bend in the arm. If the bowler uses a stepped approach, they should continue to maintain this feel throughout the approach and delivery.

The approach and delivery will be similar to those described earlier in Chapters 5, 6, 7 and 8.

After the spotter relays which pins are left, the bowler will move sideways from their previous position, either closer to or further away from the rail, until the bowing arm is in line with the key pin of the spare.

Without a Rail

When bowling without a rail, bowlers use the same physical approach and delivery as discussed in previous chapters; the difference is in the method of lining up.

To line up without a rail or a spotter, the bowler will place their leg against the ball return and take a well-practiced sidestep or two; this will position them in the desired place on the approach. Since a pair of lanes share a ball return, for the bowler to get in the same position on each lane they need to practice both left and right sidesteps as these steps may differ in length. Also, when visiting other centers, it is important to find out where the ball returns are positioned as they may be a different distance from the foul line.

Other Adaptive Techniques and Equipment

Depending on a bowler's ability to hold the ball with one hand or to use a stepped approach, there are some additional skills which can be used. These skills will be discussed in the next chapter in the context of adaptations for young or senior bowlers. However, the techniques can be used for bowlers of all ages who have various limitations.

There are two additional pieces of adaptive equipment that are commonly used by bowlers. These are the snap-handle ball and the ball pusher.

The snap-handle ball consists of a ball of regulation size and weight but imbedded in the surface of the ball is a handle which is pulled up when ready to use. As the bowler releases this ball, springs pull the handle back into the surface of the ball, leaving it flush with the surface to meet USBC requirements *(Figure 13-4)*.

The ball pusher is a bar with a handle on one end and either prongs or a "cup" on the other end. The bowler will place the ball on the approach near, but not over, the foul line. Holding the handle, the bowler puts the prongs or cup against the ball and then pushes to make the ball go down the lane *(Figure 13-4)*. If the bar comes down and touches the lane beyond the foul line, it will be considered a foul.

Figure 13-4, Snap-handle ball and Ball Pusher

YOUTH AND SENIORS

A Lifetime Sport

Bowling is a lifetime activity that can boast of having some of the youngest and oldest participants of any sport. Not only can people of all ages bowl, but it's one of the few sports where various age groups can compete with each other. This chapter provides ideas to help young and senior bowlers.

Techniques for Young Bowlers

Often, when young people start to bowl they do not have the physical coordination necessary to deliver a bowling ball properly. But there are ways that young bowlers can keep the ball on the lane, knock down pins and have fun.

Even the youngest bowlers can begin to learn the basics of the sport and some important life lessons, such as how to take turns. They also learn about strikes, spares, the foul line and safety issues. However, the most important thing a young bowler needs to learn is how to have fun and enjoy the sport.

There's no set age to begin bowling as it really depends on how big and strong a child is and how easily they can handle a bowling ball. Besides being able to physically roll the ball, the child's ability to concentrate also is an important factor.

While the ability to concentrate is something that can best be judged by parents, there is a test for physical strength. If the child can pick up the ball from the ball return and carry it by themselves to the foul line, this is approximately the same amount of strength necessary for them to push the ball with both hands from the foul line down to the pins.

Starting Ball Weight

Generally, a youth bowler can start with a ball that is approximately 10 percent of their body weight. For example, a bowler who weighs about 70 pounds would start with a seven-pound ball. Young bowlers with well-developed strength and coordination may be able to use a ball that is slightly heavier. If the bowler is having difficulty controlling the ball, change to a lighter ball.

Two-Handed Delivery

Properly learning the two-handed delivery can establish some skills that will be useful as the bowler develops and gets older.

For the basic two-handed delivery, the bowler should start with the ball being lined up with the center dot at the foul line. This center dot is slightly larger than the others and young bowlers can easily find the "big" dot.

Figure 14-1, PeeWee Push

Position the ball so that the holes face upward with the finger and thumb holes to the side or parallel to the foul line. The reason for this is because most bowling balls have a weight block and can be slightly heavier between the span. If this heavy spot is angled to the right or left, it can cause the ball to roll in that direction. Having the fingers and thumb to the sides also will allow the ball to roll between the finger and thumb holes without hitting them. If the ball rolls over the holes it can cause the ball to "jump" and go off the intended path.

Once in the proper position, the bowler will stand with their feet approximately shoulder-width apart. Have the bowler squat down or, if they are strong enough, have them hold the ball with both hands between their legs *(Figure 14-1)*.

When the bowler is ready, have them give the ball a big push or swing it between their legs and follow through straight up overhead (Figure 14-1). Be sure the bowler follows through with both hands.

Two-Handed Approach

More young bowlers are using a two-handed approach in which they deliver the ball much like a traditional style but use two hands to support the ball during the swing and approach. Jason Belmonte of Australia has had success in professional events using this style. By using two hands during the swing and approach, young bowlers are able to better support the ball.

Placement of the hands

Using finger and thumb holes: Using their dominant hand, the bowler places fingers first into the ball, followed by the thumb (Refer to Chapter 3). In the stance, the bowler's dominant hand will be under the ball with the non-bowling hand positioned directly across on top of the ball. This helps support the weight during the swing. Just prior to the release, the non-bowling hand will leave the ball and continue out to their side for balance. The dominant hand releases the ball with the thumb first followed by the fingers.

Using finger holes only: Bowler places fingers of dominant hand into the ball, and then places their palm on the ball with their thumb on the outside of the ball (Refer to Chapter 3). In the stance, the bowler's dominant hand will be under the ball with the non-bowling hand positioned directly across on top of the ball. This helps support the weight during the swing. Just prior to the release, the non-bowling hand will leave the ball and continue out to their side for balance. The dominant hand releases the ball with the ball rolling off their palm first followed by the fingers.

No holes drilled in ball: Since there are no holes drilled in the ball, the bowler will lay their dominate hand on the ball. In the stance, the bowler's dominant hand will be under the ball with the non-bowling hand positioned directly across on top of the ball to help support the weight during the swing. Just prior to the release, the non-bowling hand will leave the ball and continue out to their side for balance. The dominant hand rolls the ball off their palm followed by the fingers. **Note:** Please refer to the specs and certification manual found on BOWL.com for more information on ball drilling and two-handed techniques.

Two-handed Staggered Stance Approach

At the foul line, the bowler will place their non ball-side foot one dot to the left or right of the center dot (right-handers will go left of the center dot, left-handers will go right of the center dot). Their ball-side foot will be 6-18 inches behind their non ball-side foot and they keep their body facing the intended target path (the third arrow is recommended). The ball is placed at hip level with their thumb pointing toward the pins; at this point the bowler should be in a balanced position. They will start the swing using both hands to guide the ball back past their hip. As the ball comes forward, just prior to the release, the non-bowling hand will leave the ball and continue out to their side for balance. The dominant hand will then roll the ball and finish with a follow-through toward the target *(Figure 14-2)*.

Two-Handed Walk and Roll

Once a bowler can successfully deliver a two-handed shot using the staggered stance approach, they should then try using a walk-and-roll method, which can be incorporated into a four or five-step approach. To start, the bowler should establish the number of steps to be used. The locator dots on the approach will be used for their starting position. The bowler will line up with their non ball-side foot one dot to the left or right of the center dot (right-handers will go left of the center dot, left-handers will go right of the center dot). Once in their stance, the bowler will place the ball at hip level and get into an athletic pose. The thumb of the hand with the ball should point toward the pins. To avoid injury, the bowler should walk – not run – to the foul line. As the bowler approaches the foul line they will swing the ball back with two hands past their hip. As the

Figure 14-2, PeeWee Two Handed Staggered Stance

ball comes forward, just prior to the release, the non-bowling hand will leave the ball and continue out to their side for balance, and the dominant hand will then roll the ball and finish with a follow-through toward the target (*Figure 14-3*).

One-handed delivery

Once bowlers are able to hold the ball with one hand, coaches can help them learn the fundamentals of swinging and rolling the ball using only one hand.

Staggered Stance

without a Push-Away

The bowler will line up with their non ball-side foot one dot to the left or right of the center dot (right-handers will go left of the center dot, left-handers will go right of the center dot). The non ball-side foot should be placed behind the ball-side foot to where they can hold their balance (6 to 18 inches back). Once in a balanced position, they should bend the knees slightly and lean a little forward from the waist.

The ball will be held down to their side with the thumb pointing toward the pins (*Figure 14-4*). Another way of looking at the hand position is that the thumb points at 12 o'clock on a clock face, just like the straight ball position discussed in Chapters 5 and 7.

The bowler will push the ball out, let the ball swing back easily and then forward (*Figure 14-4*). At the bottom of the swing, they will release the ball toward their intended target (the center arrow is recommended). Make sure there is only one swing as multiple swings may cause the ball to start swinging sideways.

There are many other skills that a youth bowler can learn as they develop strength and coordination. As young bowlers become more interested in bowling, it is recommended that parents find a USBC youth bowling program with USBC certified coaches who are trained to help bowlers further develop their skills.

Figure 14-3, Two-handed walk and roll

Figure 14-4, Staggered stance without a push-away

Techniques for Senior Bowlers

"You're never too old to bowl" is a familiar saying. With the growing number of senior leagues throughout the country, this couldn't be more true. As people become older, the knees hurt more, they can't bend as much, and it becomes more difficult for bowlers to bowl like they once did. Fortunately, there are some physical adjustments that can be made that will help bowlers continue to enjoy bowling for many more years. In addition to the ideas that follow in this section, there is also some valuable information in the previous chapters that can help the senior bowler adjust.

Ball Weight and Grip

Senior bowlers that want to increase accuracy and power should use a ball that is lighter than what they once used. Because the ball is not as heavy, the armswing can remain free and loose instead of forced.

As discussed in other chapters, this good armswing is important to consistency and accuracy.

Bowlers also can change the grip, making it easier to hold and release. As bowlers get older, the fingers and thumb size change, joints can swell and the span can change. An IBPSIA trained pro shop operator can help bowlers evaluate the span and hole sizes to decide if there are any adjustments necessary.

Bowlers who have been using a ball with a fingertip grip may want to switch to a conventional grip. This isn't required unless the bowlers hand and fingers begin to hurt while bowling. Senior bowlers can have extra grip holes drilled in the ball for their index and pinky fingers, these extra holes are perfectly legal and can make it much easier to hold, swing and release the ball.

Modified Approach

There are other changes to the approach that can make it easier to deliver the ball effectively. The two main components of the physical game that are most important to maintain are the armswing and balance.

Figure 14-5, Staggered stance with a push-away

Figure 14-6, One Step

For example, if a bowler needs to reduce their knee bend to stay balanced, then they should reduce the knee bend. If the wrist cannot support the weight of the ball and it affects the armswing, the bowler should consider using a wrist device.

If it becomes difficult for bowlers to use a standard approach, the approach can be modified. Two recommendations are using the staggered stance with a push-away. In this delivery the bowler will not use any steps; the other recommendation is to use the one-step approach which uses the last step of the traditional approach.

Staggered Stance with a Push-Away

The staggered stance without a push-away, or no-step delivery, is described earlier in this chapter in the youth section. Another method that seniors can use is the Staggered Stance with a Push-away *(Figure 14-5)*. They start at the foul line with their non ball-side foot on the center dot. The non ball-side foot should be placed behind the ball-side foot to where they can hold their balance (6 to 18 inches back). Once in a balanced position, they should bend the knees slightly and lean a little forward from the waist.

They will hold the ball waist-high between their chin and shoulder. To deliver the ball, the bowler pushes the ball out toward their target and lets the ball swing easily back and forward, releasing the ball at the bottom of the swing as it passes the ankle of the non ball-side leg finishing with a follow through.

One Step Approach

For the one-step approach, the bowler stands one and a half steps back from the foul line *(Figure 14-6)*. They set up in the stance (athletic pose) as described in Chapter 5. When ready, they push the ball out and down, letting the ball swing easily back. As the ball begins to swing forward, the bowler will step or slide forward with their non ball-side foot and release the ball as it passes the ankle of the non ball-side leg finishing with a follow through.

International Bowling Campus

International Bowling Campus (IBC)

621 Six Flags Drive
Arlington, TX 76011

The International Bowling Campus includes the following organizations: United States Bowling Congress, Bowling Proprietors' Association of America, the International Bowling Museum and Hall of Fame, the International Training and Research Center, Strike Ten Entertainment, The Bowling Foundation, International Bowling Pro Shop and Instructors Association, the Billiard and Bowling Institute of America, the Bowling News Network and the Bowling Writers' Association of America.

A Look at the Organizations at the IBC

United States Bowling Congress (USBC)

(800) 514-BOWL
www.BOWL.com

The United States Bowling Congress is the national governing body for the sport of bowling as recognized by the United States Olympic Committee. The organization provides member services to bowlers and leagues, including standardized playing rules and awards for various achievements. USBC also ensures the integrity of the sport and manages many behind-the-scenes tasks to help bowlers enjoy the sport. USBC coordinates the selection and activities of Team USA and Junior Team USA for international competition.

USBC was created in January 2005 through the merger of the American Bowling Congress, Women's International Bowling Congress, Young American Bowling Alliance and USA Bowling.

The USBC has many departments to provide specialized assistance to the bowling community. The USBC mission is to ensure the integrity and protect the future of the sport, provide programs and services, and enhance the bowling experience.

Bowling Proprietors' Association of America (BPAA)

(800)343-1329
www.bpaa.com

The Bowling Proprietors' Association of America is a non-profit membership organization for those who own and operate bowling centers. The organization provides services to members such as group-buying discounts, promotional ideas and tips for operating a successful bowling center. Its mission is to enhance the profitability of its member centers and its vision is to be an essential resource to bowling centers and to lead a united, growing, more prosperous and highly-regarded bowling industry.

International Training and Research Center (ITRC)

(800) 514-BOWL ext. 8222
www.bowlingitrc.com

This state-of-the-art facility is equipped with 14 dedicated training lanes where athletes can use video analysis, ball-tracking systems, biomechanical motion tracking, and state-of-the-art robotics along with foot-

International Training and Research Center

International Bowling Museum and Hall of Fame

and grip-pressure mapping to help improve their game. The training center has a staff of world-class coaches, a top-of-the-line pro shop and a fully-equipped fitness center. It also is the home training center for Team USA and Junior Team USA. The ITRC has six lanes dedicated to testing and research.

International Bowling Museum and Hall of Fame (IBM/HF)

(817) 649-5105
www.bowlingmuseum.com

The International Bowling Museum and Hall of Fame brings to life the colorful, 5,000-year history of the sport. The museum has a vast collection of historical artifacts and also features interactive presentations. The Hall of Fame section honors the legends of the game, past and present, and also has interactive displays.

International Bowling Pro Shop and Instructors Association (IBPSIA)

(800) 514-2695
www.ibpsia.com

The International Bowling Pro Shop and Instructors Association was founded in 1991. Pro shop professionals and instructors are trained to analyze a bowler's game so they can customize equipment and grip, based on a bowler's skill level. Its mission is to provide education, communication, and recognition for bowling pro shop professionals and instructors, creating a foundation for the advancement of the worldwide bowling industry.

Strike Ten Entertainment (STE)

(800) 871-7869
www.stemarketing.com

Strike Ten Entertainment, part of the BPAA, is the marketing arm of the bowling industry. Its mission is to increase the number of paid bowling games in centers each year and attract and build long-term relationships with national corporate and marketing sponsors.

The Bowling Foundation

(888)302-8122
www.bowlingfoundation.org

The Bowling Foundation is the charitable arm for the sport of bowling. It assists selected charities in the United States and internationally that have appeal to society, bowlers, the industry and sport in general. By reaching out to bowlers, bowling center management and proprietors, bowling equipment manufacturers, retailers and their partners, The Bowling Foundation helps to promote these causes, raise awareness and funding.

The Billiard and Bowling Institute of America (BBIA)

(800) 343-1329
www.billiardandbowling.org

The not-for-profit association was formed in Chicago in 1940 to service the billiard and bowling industries. It is comprised of leading bowling and billiard manufacturers, independent bowling distributors and major billiard retailers.

Other National Organizations

The National Bowling Association

9944 Reading Road
Evandale, Ohio 45241
(513) 769-1985
www.tnbainc.org

The National Bowling Association was formed in 1939 by African-American bowlers but is open to all who wish to join. TNBA conducts tournaments, provides awards and scholarships, and publishes TNBA Bowler magazine for its members.

Special Olympics

1133 19th Street, N.W.
Washington, D.C. 20036
(202) 628-3630
www.specialolympics.org

Special Olympics, founded by Eunice Kennedy in 1968, is a worldwide program of sports training and competition for athletes with cognitive challenges. Supported by more than 500,000 volunteers, Special Olympics has chapters in all 50 states and more than 120 countries.

Special Olympics training and competition takes place year-round in both summer and winter events. Approximately 500,000 athletes participate in bowling, making it the second-largest Special Olympics sport behind track and field.

USBC annually hosts a national Special Olympics Unified Tournament prior to the start of the USBC Open Championships tournament. Unified Sports is a pioneer program that puts Special Olympics athletes and more experienced athletes with mental retardation together on the same team. As their averages improve, Special Olympians can be moved by their coaches to compete as non-Special Olympics partners.

Special Olympics volunteers always are needed. Contact your local Special Olympics chapter for more information.

Bowlers to Veterans Link

11350 Random Hills Road, Suite 800
Fairfax, VA 22030
(703) 934-6039
www.bowlforveterans.org

Each year, Bowlers to Veterans Link provides patients at Veterans Administration medical centers with programs and equipment to help speed recovery and boost their spirits. It accomplishes this through cash grants for recreational equipment, touring entertainment troupes, sponsorship of visiting celebrity bowlers and much more.

CAREER OPPORTUNITIES IN BOWLING

From the friendly competitions that can be found at local bowling centers, to the high-profile events that are seen on television, bowling has it all. There are numerous opportunities that a bowler can pursue, from being an amateur bowler on the weekends, a touring professional bowler or getting a job in the bowling industry.

Amateur Competition

Bowling remains one of the fastest-growing high school sports, according to the National Federation of State High School Associations. Local school systems and states are adding programs at both the club and varsity levels. High school bowling provides a great opportunity for bowlers to develop their skills while representing their schools in competition.

Colleges around the country also are adding bowling as a sport at an unprecedented rate. Starting with the 2003-04 season, the NCAA officially recognized women's bowling as a championship sport. College bowling provides athletes opportunities for scholarships and to become national champions.

The ultimate in competition is to become a member of Team USA, an elite group of top amateur and professional athletes who represent the United States in prestigious events all over the world. Team USA and Junior Team USA members are among the most visible ambassadors for the sport. Team USA, funded and operated by the United States Bowling Congress, is comprised of a minimum of 10 men and 10 women from the amateur and professional bowling ranks. The top three men and top three women athletes at the annual USBC Team USA Trials, a grueling tournament consisting of four nine-game blocks over four days on four different and challenging lane oil patterns, earn automatic berths on Team USA. Two additional men and two women are chosen from the field by the National Selection Committee after an extensive analysis of their physical and mental games as well as their past performances and team-play abilities. The committee will also choose a minimum of five men and

five women from the PBA Tour or Team USA Members within the last 10 years to be on the current team.

USBC Junior Team USA also consists of 10 males and 10 females. The top four male and top four female finishers at the USBC Junior Gold Championships earn spots on the team and the National Selection Committee picks two male and two female athletes from the match-play portion of the Junior Gold Championships. The top two males and top two females age 20 and under as of January 1 who bowl in the USBC Team Trials, provided they are not already on the team, earn spots on Junior Team USA. The final spots are determined by the National Selection Committee from a pool of athletes that were either match-play finalists at the Junior Gold Championships or competed at the USBC Team Trials. Athletes selected from the Team Trials can be USBC Youth or Adult members as long as they meet the age requirement. More information on Team USA can be found at the USBC website, BOWL.com.

Competitive bowlers also can find a variety of tournaments that range from local events to tournaments that draw participants from around the world. Some of these events offer relatively small prize amounts while others fall into the "mega-bucks" category.

Professional Competition

There are two levels of professional competition. Most people are familiar with the men's and women's tournaments that are on national television, but there are regional competitions as well.

The regional tours offer the high-average bowler an opportunity to compete in a challenging environment on demanding lane conditions. Those who do well in the regional tours will often go out and compete on the national tour.

The Professional Bowlers Association provides elite bowlers with tour events and a high level of competition in the United States and abroad. These events are televised on a regular basis.

Industry Opportunities

There are opportunities in the bowling industry with the two major sources being bowling center operations and the manufacturers that supply goods and services to bowlers and bowling centers.

Bowling Center Operations

Bowling centers have a variety of positions available for those who are interested in a career in the sport. Some are the front-line customer service positions at the control counter, restaurant and lounge. Others work behind the scenes, such as maintenance and repair technicians who work on the machines that set the pins.

Management positions also are available and managing a center requires different skills and talents. Centers have a variety of customers, from recreational players to highly-skilled competitors, and there also is food and beverage management, service management, business, marketing and facility management.

Multi-center chains employ people with a wider range of skills such as accounting, purchasing, marketing, and computer specialists.

Coaching

Coaching is another growing trend in center operations. Center owners and managers understand that the more knowledgeable bowlers become, the more often they will bowl. While many coaches volunteer with youth and other programs, others earn an income giving private lessons, running camps and clinics, and coaching high school or college teams. USBC Coaching provides educational materials directly to bowlers as well as providing training for coaches and bowling centers.

Pro Shop Operator

Pro shop operators help bowlers with ball selection, custom fitting of bowling balls, accessories and offer lessons. IBPSIA provides education, communication and recognition for those interested in owning or working in a pro shop. USBC Coaching provides coaching certifications to keep them current on the latest developments in bowling technology.

Manufacturers

Bowling manufacturers that supply equipment to pro shops and bowling centers employ a wide range of people. As with any business, these companies have departments such as human resources, marketing and operations, materials management, building maintenance, warehouse management, marketing, computer/IT and various manufacturing positions. Most companies that supply equipment in the bowling industry also maintain sales departments with regional sales representatives who call on centers, distributors and pro shops with information about their products and services.

International Bowling Campus

In addition to employment opportunities within the bowling industry as an athlete, coach, pro shop owner/operator or manufacturer, there are opportunities within organizations at the International Bowling Campus. For current position vacancies, visit the website, BOWL.com.

Bowlers that become involved with leagues will find that the heart of USBC can be found in its local and state volunteer associations. These volunteers are the backbone of bowling management. Local and state associations manage the day-to-day services that are provided. These associations start membership processing, distribute awards, certify that lanes and equipment are within standards, and conduct various tournaments for their members.

Professional Bowler Chris Barnes

GLOSSARY OF BOWLING TERMS

- A -

ABC - American Bowling Congress, founded in 1895, was one of four organizations that merged to form the United States Bowling Congress on Jan. 1, 2005. At one time, ABC was the world's largest sports membership organization. With the Women's International Bowling Congress (WIBC), ABC was an official rules-making body of tenpin bowling in the United States, Puerto Rico and military bases worldwide.

ACTUAL – See SCRATCH

ABSENT – A score used in league when a bowler on the team is not there to bowl.

ADJUST - When a bowler changes his/her starting point on the approach and/or target on the lane.

ALLEY – See LANE

ALL-EVENTS – In a tournament, the combined total score of singles, doubles and team events.

ANCHOR - Last player in a lineup for team competition.

ANGULAR MOVE – An adjustment where the starting position on the approach is changed and the lane target either remains the same or is moved a different amount, resulting in a different angle.

APPROACH – 1) Portion of the lane behind the foul line used by bowlers to build momentum to deliver the ball. 2) The movement of a bowler from stance to the delivery.

AREA - The margin of error where the bowler can miss their target and still hit the pocket.

ARROWS - Targets on the lane starting about 15 feet from the foul line.

ASSOCIATIONS - Name applied to volunteer organizations serving at the local and state levels for USBC.

AVERAGE – For a bowler, the total number of pins knocked down divided by the number of games bowled.

- B -

BABY SPLIT – A split where there is one pin missing between those left. For example, the 2-7, 3-10, 4-5, 5-6 splits.

BACK UP – See REVERSE HOOK

BACKEND – The last 15 feet of the lane before the pins.

BAKER SYSTEM - A format that calls for different players bowling in different frames. Mainly used in five-person team competition where the number 1 bowler throws in the first and sixth frames, the number 2 bowler in the second and seventh, etc.

BALL – The object rolled at the pins in order to knock them down.

BALL RETURN - 1) The machine that returns the ball to the player. 2) Where the ball rests on or near the approach.

BALL RACK – Storage structure where establishments keep house balls.

BALL TRACK – 1) The portion of the ball that comes in contact with the lane surface. 2) The area on the lane where the majority of balls are rolled creating a worn path.

BIG FOUR – A split resulting in the 4, 6, 7 and 10 pins still standing after the first shot.

BLIND - Score allowed for absent member, usually lower than his/her average as a penalty.

BLOCK – 1) A term to describe an easy lane condition. 2) A specific squad or time bowled.

BLOW THE RACK – Expression that applies to a variety of strikes, especially a light, sweeping strike.

BOARD - Wooden lanes have boards approximately one-inch wide Synthetic lanes feature the same image. Bowlers use specific boards to line up their stance and as their target on various shots.

BONUS – Extra pins or points awarded during match-play competition for winning a particular match.

BOWLER'S AREA (Also SETTEE) – The area where players wait between shots. Usually contains seats and a scoring unit.

BOWLING CENTER – A facility where people go to bowl.

BRACKETS FORMAT – In a tournament, where bowlers or teams are paired to compete and the winner advances to bowl other winners. This continues until there is only one bowler or team left undefeated.

BREAKDOWN – 1) The change or deterioration of the initial oil pattern. 2) Malfunction of the pinsetter or ball return

BREAK POINT - Place on the lane where the ball begins to hook toward the pins.

BRIDGE - The area between the finger holes on a bowling ball.

BROOKLYN (Also CROSSOVER) – Describes a strike ball that goes to the opposite side it was intended. For example, a right-hander hitting the left side of the head pin. (In Brooklyn, it is called a "Jersey.")

BUCKET – A term used to describe the 2-4-5-8 or 3-5-6-9 spare leaves.

- C -

CARRY DOWN – The oil that is moved, or transferred, down the lane from bowling balls.

CERTIFICATION – 1) Competition registered with and conducted in accordance with USBC rules. All certified bowling centers must have their lanes inspected by USBC annually to ensure they meet specifications. 2) The accreditation earned by USBC coaches upon completion of training courses.

CHANNEL (Also GUTTER) - The 10-inch out-of-bounds area to the right and left of the lane that guides the ball to the pit once it leaves the playing area.

CHAMPIONSHIP FORMAT – A tournament format usually run for local, state and national tournaments consisting of multiple events.

CHOP (Also CHERRY and PICK) – To hit the front pin of a spare leave while the pin behind or alongside remains standing.

CLASSIFIED - Leagues or tournaments with average limitations or other restrictions.

CLEAN GAME - A game with a spare or strike in each frame.

CLOSED SHOULDERS – When a bowler's shoulders remain parallel with the foul line or return to this position from being open. See also open shoulders.

CONCOURSE – The main walkway and spectator area in a bowling center; where food and drinks should be kept.

CONDITIONER – See LANE CONDITIONER

CONTROL DESK – The main hub in a bowling center where all lane activity is managed.

CONVENTIONAL GRIP – The grip in which the fingers are inserted into the second knuckle and the thumb fully inserted; recommended for beginning bowlers.

CONVERT - Knock down the remaining pins on the lane for a spare.

COUNT - Number of pins knocked down on each ball.

CORE - The interior of a bowling ball.

COVERSTOCK (Also SHELL) A term referring to the outside of the bowling ball. Specifically, the material from which it was made.

CROSSLANE – 1) The concept of the starting position being on the opposite side of the approach from where the spare leave stands. For example, standing on the far left side of the lane to throw at the number 10 pin. 2) Alternating between two lanes in different frames.

CROSSOVER – See BROOKLYN

CUSHION - The padding at the rear of the pit to absorb the shock of the ball and pins.

- D -

DEAD BALL (Also FLAT BALL) – 1) An ineffective ball that deflects badly when it hits the pins. 2) Can be declared at delivery if any of a variety of factors occurs as listed in the USBC Rule Book. 3) Any ball that enters the channel.

DEAD WOOD – Pins that fall over but remain on the lane or in the channel that must be removed before the next shot.

DEFLECTION - The movement of the ball after it hits the pins.

DELIVERY - The combination of a bowler's approach and release.

DOTS – See Locator Dots.

DOUBLE - Two consecutive strikes.

DOUBLES EVENT – A team of two players, usually in a tournament.

DOUBLE WOOD (Also SLEEPER) - When one pin is directly behind the other. For example, the 1-5, 2-8 or 3-9.

DRIFT – A bowler's inability to finish in the same spot at the foul line.

DRY LANE - A lane that has a little amount of conditioner (oil).

DUROMETER TEST - An instrument that inserts a needle into the ball's surface to determine its hardness.

DUTCH 200 - A 200 game scored by alternating strikes and spares.

- E -

ELIMINATION FORMAT – In a tournament, after a game or series of games have been bowled, bowler(s) with the lowest scores are eliminated.

- F -

FAST EIGHT - A high pocket hit that leaves the 4-7 for a right-hander or the 6-10 for a left-hander.

FILL - Pins knocked down following a spare or two consecutive strikes in the 10th frame.

FINGERTIP GRIP – The grip in which the fingers are inserted to the first knuckle and thumb fully inserted; recommended for experienced bowlers.

FIT – Relating to the way a hand fits in the bowling ball.

FLAT BALL – See DEAD BALL

FLUSH (Also PACK) – When a ball hits the pocket solid for a strike.

FOUL - Going beyond the foul line at delivery. Results in a zero scored for that delivery.

FOUL LINE – A solid black stripe which separates the approach from the lane.

FOUNDATION FRAME - The ninth frame. The desire is to roll a strike or spare as a "foundation" for the 10th frame.

FRAME - Each game is divided into 10 frames, the first nine allowing a maximum of two shots with three shots allowed in the 10th frame.

FRONTS (Also HEADS) - The first 15 feet of the lane beyond the foul line.

FULL ROLLER - A ball that rolls over its full circumference and produces a track between the thumb and fingers.

- G -

GREEK CHURCH - The 4-6-7-8-10 (LH) or 4-6-7-9-10 (RH) leave.

GRIP – The way the hand fits in the ball. Either conventional or fingertip.

GUTTER – See CHANNEL

- H -

HANDICAP - Pins given to individuals or teams in an attempt to equalize the competition.

HEADS – See FRONTS

HEAD PIN - The 1-pin.

HIGH HIT - A ball that makes contact near the center of the head pin on a strike attempt.

HITTING UP – Releasing the ball late on the upswing.

HOLD – An area on the lane that resists hook action of the ball, preventing it from hooking high on the head pin.

HOOK – 1) A ball path that usually curves sharply near the pins. 2) The second phase of ball motion.

HOOKING LANE - A lane on which the ball has more tendency to curve or hook.

HOUSE – A term for a bowling center.

HOUSE BALL - Bowling ball provided by the center.

HOUSE SHOES - Rental shoes provided by the center.

HOUSE SHOT (Also HOUSE CONDITION) – The oil pattern typically used by bowling centers for leagues and other events.

- I -

INSIDE - A line used by a bowler who plays toward the center of the lane such as the third, fourth or fifth arrows.

- J -

JUNIOR TEAM USA – The official USBC team comprised of male and female bowlers age 20 and under who represent the United States in international competition.

- K -

KEGLER - German word for bowler. The term was used to describe bowlers for many years.

KEY PIN – In spare shooting, it is the pin that the ball must initially hit to convert the spare.

KICKBACK - Vertical division boards between lanes in the pit. On most hits, the pins bounce off the kickbacks to knock down additional pins.

- L -

LABEL - The manufacturer's marking on the ball, pin or lane.

LANE (Also ALLEY) – Playing surface made of either maple and pine wood or a synthetic surface.

LANE CONDITIONER (Also LANE OIL or LANE DRESSING) - An oil used to coat or dress the lanes, necessary to protect the lane surface. Also affects the reaction of a bowling ball.

LANE FINISH – A Urethane based product placed on wood lanes to protect the lanes surface.

LEADOFF - First player in a team lineup.

LEAGUE – A competition where bowlers or teams of bowlers compete against others in a series of weeks or sessions.

LEVERAGE - Being in the proper posture position at the foul line with the knee solidly under the body to allow maximum strength in rolling the ball. 2) A type of drilling layout for a bowling ball.

LIGHT – Describes a shot that is not fully in the pocket. For a right-hander, too much to the right.

LINE – 1) The path a bowling ball takes from release to the pins. 2) One game of bowling.

LOCATOR DOTS (Also DOTS) – 1) Markings imbedded in the lane just past the foul line and used by some bowlers as their target. 2) A series of dots on the approach used to assist the bowler in lining up on the approach.

LOFT – The distance beyond the foul line that the ball travels after leaving the bowler's hand to the point of impact on the lane surface.

- M -

MAPLE – Very hard wood used in the front of the lanes, approaches and bowling pins.

MARK – 1) Getting a strike or spare in a frame. 2) The spot on the lane bowlers use as their target.

MATCH PLAY - Portion of tournament or league play where bowlers are competing one on one.

MESSENGER - A pin that goes back across the lane bed to knock down additional pins.

MIDLANE (Also PINES) – The 30-foot section between the fronts and back end.

MISS – See OPEN

MIXED LEAGUES – Leagues of men and women competing together.

MIXER - A hit that causes the pins to bounce around.

- N -

NO TAP - A form of competition that awards a strike when nine pins are knocked down on the first ball. It also can be when eight pins are knocked down.

NOSE HIT - When the ball hits the front center of the head pin.

- O -

OIL – See LANE CONDITIONER

OILY (Also SLICK) - Indicates that there is a heavy coating of conditioner on the lane, making it difficult to hook the ball.

OPEN (Also MISS) – A frame that doesn't include a strike or spare.

OPEN BOWLING - Non-league, non-tournament play, practice.

OPEN SHOULDERS – When a bowler's shoulder is turned toward the ball side.

OUTSIDE – Rolling the ball starting from an area close to the channel, such as the first arrow.

OVER - In tournament play, 200 is often used for "par." If an individual is averaging over that figure, he/she is considered over for that tournament. Example: Bowler has a score of 652 for 3 games; par would be 600 so they are 52 over for the tournament.

- P -

PARTICLE BALLS – Developed in the mid-1990s, bowling balls made using high-tech manufacturing processes to insert minute pieces of silica such as glass beads in the ball's shell to increase hook potential.

PACK – See FLUSH

PARALLEL MOVE – An adjustment where the starting position and lane target are moved the same amount and in the same direction.

PERFECT GAME - Rolling 12 consecutive strikes in one game for a score of 300.

PLASTIC BALLS - Developed during the 1950s and made of polyester.

PICK – See SPARE or CHOP

PIN – The free-standing targets at the end of the lane. They are set in groups of 10 for each frame.

PIN ACTION – Pins that bounce or roll around the pin deck knocking down other pins.

PIN DECK - The area at the end of the lane where the pins are set.

PINFALL – The total count of pins knocked over in a given shot, series of shots or games.

PIN TRIANGLE – The arrangement of pins sitting on the pin deck.

PINES – See MIDLANE

PIT - Open area behind the pin deck where pins and balls go after leaving the back of the pin deck.

PITCH - Angle at which holes are drilled into a bowling ball.

POCKET - Where a ball hits solidly between the 1-pin and 3-pin for right-handers and the 1-pin and 2-pin for left-handers.

POLISH – A compound used to shine bowling balls in order to decrease hook potential.

POSITION ROUNDS – Part of leagues or tournaments when teams or players face each other based on their standings. Example: First place meets second, third meets fourth, etc.

POT GAME – Competition in which two or more bowlers post some sort of stake on a winner-take-all basis or to be divided by the number of entrants.

PUNCH OUT - Refers to getting three strikes in the 10th frame.

- Q -

QUALIFYING FORMAT – In a tournament, when bowlers bowl a set number of games attempting to advance to the next round.

- R -

READING THE LANES – Observation of the overall ball reaction to determine the best place to roll the ball for a strike.

RELEASE – The point at which a bowler lets go of the ball.

RELEASE POINT – The moment the bowler releases the ball with the thumb, rolling off the fingers and imparting rotation to the ball.

RESIN BALLS - Developed in the 1990s, made of an advanced urethane. Resin bowling balls increase hook potential.

RESURFACE – 1) when a center cuts the worn out damaged parts of a wood lane down to the bare wood in preparation for re coating the lane finish. 2) When a pro shop resurfaces a bowling ball removing cuts, scratches and wear and tear from the coverstock.

REVERSE HOOK (Also BACKUP) – A ball that hooks toward the hand from which the bowler delivered it. For example, a right-hander who hooks the ball to the right.

REVOLUTIONS - Also known as "revs." The amount of rotation a bowler imparts to a bowling ball as it travels from the foul line to the pins.

ROLL OUT – A ball that stops hooking and begins to go straight.

- S -

SANDBAGGER - Bowler who purposely keeps his/her average down to receive a higher handicap.

SANDING – A process used on bowling balls to increase hook potential.

SCOTCH DOUBLES – A competition where two partners alternate shots during a game.

SCRATCH (Also ACTUAL) – Bowling score that does not include any handicap.

SEMI ROLLER - A ball that rolls off its center and produces a track outside of the thumb and fingers.

SET – 1) Ball holding into the pocket. 2) A series of games.

SETTEE – See BOWLERS AREA

SHELL – See COVERSTOCK

SHOT – 1) A single delivery 2) Reference to where to play specific types of oil patterns.

SINGLES EVENT – When one person competes against all others, in his/her division, usually in a tournament.

SKID – The first phase of ball motion when the ball slides though the front portion of the lane.

SLEEPER – See DOUBLE WOOD

SLICK – See OILY

SNOWPLOW - A ball that hits straight on the head pin and clears the pins for a strike.

SPAN - The distance between the thumb and finger holes on a bowling ball.

SPARE - Knocking down all 10 pins in two shots.

SPLICE – On wood lanes, the way the hard and soft wood parts of the lane come together.

SPLIT - A spare leave in which the head pin is down and the remaining combination of pins have a gap between them, ranging from the 4-5 to the 7-10.

SPOT - A target on the lane surface at which the bowler aims, ranging from a dot to an arrow to a board or area.

SQUARE – A reference to having the shoulders, hips or body parallel to the foul line.

STANCE – The balanced starting position that bowlers assume before making their approach and delivery.

STEPLADDER – A competition in which the lower qualifier bowls against the next-highest qualifier. This is usually done in the final phase of a competition known as stepladder finals.

STONE 10 – Leaving a 10 pin on a seemingly good first ball.

STRIKE - Knocking down all 10 pins on the first ball.

STRIKING OUT – Finishing the game with a string of consecutive strikes.

STRING - A number of continuous strikes.

SWEEPER – 1) A form of competition that usually is conducted in association with another tournament. 2) A separate competition at the end of a league.

SYNTHETIC LANE - A non-wood or manmade lane surface that may be placed over an existing wood lane or a pre-constructed unit placed on a foundation.

SYNTHETIC PINS - Non-wood or manmade pins.

- T -

TAP – A single pin that stands on a seemingly perfect strike shot.

TARGET – A mark or area of the lane which the bowler uses to aim his or her shot.

TARGETING - Selecting a spot on the lane for the ball to roll over such as the dots, the arrows, a particular board or area. Some bowlers select the pins.

TEAM USA – The official USBC team composed of men and women representing the United States in international competition.

TIMING – A measurement of where the ball is in relationship to the steps during the approach.

TOPPING THE BALL - When the fingers are on top of the ball instead of behind, below or to the side upon release.

TOURNAMENT – A competition where bowlers or teams compete in a single or series of events against all others in their division.

TRACK – 1) The worn or most used part of a lane 2) The part of the ball that contacts the lane surface when rolling.

TRACK FLARE – When a track migrates over a slightly different part of the ball with each revolution.

TURKEY - Three consecutive strikes.

TURN – 1) The hand motion that imparts rotation to a ball upon release. 2) A ball that hooks.

- U -

UNITED STATES BOWLING CONGRESS - The organization created when the American Bowling Congress, Women's International Bowling Congress, Young American Bowling Alliance and USA Bowling merged into one organization on Jan. 1, 2005.

USA BOWLING – Formerly recognized by the U.S. Olympic Committee as the organization responsible for amateur competition in the United States.

USBC COACHING – **Organization headquartered in Arlington, Texas, that** trains and certifies coaches to teach the sport of bowling. USBC Coaching is the only bowling coaching program recognized by the U.S. Olympic Committee.

UNDER - In tournament play, 200 often is used for "par" and if an individual is averaging below that figure, he/she is considered under for that tournament. Example: Bowler has a score of 550 for three games; par would be 600 so they are 50 under for the tournament.

URETHANE – A material used in making the cover of a bowling ball.

- V -

VACANCY – A score given to a team when they do not have a full roster in a league.

VISUALIZATION – A mental-game technique that helps a bowler concentrate.

- W -

WIBC - Women's International Bowling Congress, one of four organizations that merged to form the United States Bowling Congress on Jan. 1, 2005.

WASHOUT - To leave the 1-2-4-7-10, 1-2-4-10 or 1-2-10; or, for left-handers, leaving the 1-3-6-7-10, 1-3-6-7 or 1-3-7 after the first ball.

WEIGHT BLOCK – Part of the core or interior of a ball.

WOOD LANE – A lane constructed from maple and pine.

- Y -

YABA - Young American Bowling Alliance, one of four organizations that merged to form the United States Bowling Congress on Jan. 1, 2005.